Published by
Green Books
An imprint of UIT Cambridge Ltd
www.greenbooks.co.uk
PO Box 145, Cambridge CB4 1GQ, England
+44 (0) 1223 302 041

First published © 2017 in German by oekom verlag, Munich under
the titel "Das Ozeanbuch"
Translation, editing and proofreading by: Rosella Vaughan, Osanna
Vaughan & Lynette Stewart
Esther Gonstalla has asserted her moral rights under the
Copyright, Designs and Patents Act 1988.
Illustrations, front cover design, layout and infographics by
Esther Gonstalla, Erdgeschoss Grafik

ISBN: 978 085 784 477 4 (paperback)
ISBN: 978 085 784 478 1 (ePub)
ISBN: 978 085 784 479 8 (pdf)
Also available as Kindle

THE OCEAN BOOK

HOW ENDANGERED ARE OUR SEAS?

by Esther Gonstalla

"I really don't know why it is
that all of us are so committed to the sea,
except I think it's because
in addition to the fact that the sea
changes, and the light changes,
and ships change, it's because we all
came from the sea. And it is
an interesting biological fact that
all of us have in our veins the
exact same percentage of salt in our blood
that exists in the ocean, and,
therefore, we have salt in our blood,
in our sweat, in our tears. We are tied
to the ocean. And when we go back
to the sea—whether it is to sail or
to watch it—we are going back from
whence we came."

US President John F. Kennedy,
Remarks at the Dinner for the America's Cup Crews
in Newport, Rhode Island, September 14, 1962

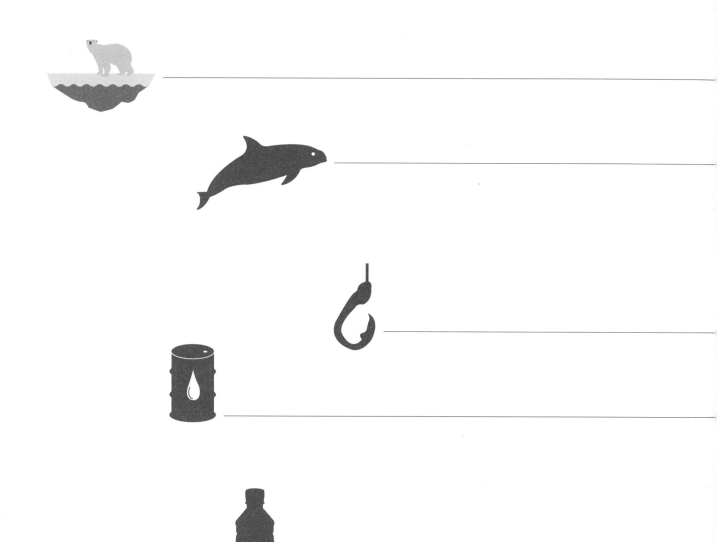

Saving our Oceans

We are currently facing a global challenge of unprecedented magnitude: saving our ocean.

Reaching beyond the borders of States and crossing continents, the ocean covers two thirds of the Planet and represents 97 % of its biosphere.

It plays a key role in the regulation of climate and produces 50 % of the oxygen we breathe, while absorbing 25 % of the world's greenhouse gas emissions. One billion people depend on seafood as their main sources of protein, algae are used in products from cosmetics to medicine and more than 80 % of the world's trade is seaborne.

However, the consequences of climate change and marine pollution are putting our ocean under severe stress. Fish stocks are being depleted because of overfishing and illegal fishing. Over 10 billion tons of litter enter the ocean every year – and every single plastic bottle takes centuries to decompose.

It is time to stop taking the preservation of our ocean for granted and to start looking after its precious resources.

My Foundation has clearly positioned the ocean among its top priorities: better understand the environmental dangers our ocean is exposed to, fight against plastic pollution, develop marine protected areas, conserve endangered species and promote innovative solutions for a sustainable ocean.

I believe that there is hope, if we work hand-in-hand. This book, which aims to raise awareness as widely as possible by explaining the issue of ocean conservation in remarkably clear terms – appealing to our sense of responsibility – is thus particularly timely. I deeply thank the author as well as the German Ocean Foundation and Geomar for this publication.

For these reasons, together with my Foundation, I want to offer support to this book and I hope that those who read it will find it as fascinating as I have.

H.S.H. Prince Albert II of Monaco

**PRINCE ALBERT II
OF MONACO
FOUNDATION**

Translated with the generous support of
The Prince Albert II of Monaco Foundation

What should the future of our oceans look like?

We humans have always lived with the oceans. We make use of them in many ways, even as we fear their enormous power, both at sea and on the coasts. For many of us, however, the ocean is not necessarily a part of our daily lives. Who thinks about the future of our oceans? Who is looking after their »health«? Oceans are being increasingly abused and polluted, especially in coastal areas. Life originated in and emerged from the oceans, and a healthy ocean is critical to sustaining life on earth. Awareness of the fact that pollution now endangers our marine environment is far from widespread.

We have always had the ocean at our service. Yet with the rapid rise of human populations, exploitation of the aquatic environment is becoming ever more intense. Questions about the future of our oceans and coastlines are becoming increasingly urgent. So how can we harmonize usage and protection?

This question seems particularly poignant in relation to fish and fisheries. Ocean fish have supplied humans in many regions with animal protein for thousands of years. In the past, fishermen often faced great peril, risking their lives to take what was needed from the ocean to provide sustenance for their communities. Thus, for a long time, the fishing industry was in balance with the ocean's ecosystems, as human need did not exceed what the ocean could spare. However, in recent years technological advancements in catching fish have caused the balance between human populations and fish populations to be lost. The current intensity of global fishing has caused the massive depletion of many fish stocks. What will the future of global fishing and our oceans look like? What should it look like?

The effects of climate change, combined with the chemical and litter pollution of our oceans, present further serious issues. As a consequence of climate change, our oceans become warmer, water levels rise, the levels of dissolved oxygen in seawater decrease, and the input of carbon dioxide turns the oceans increasingly acidic. How much pollution, especially in our coastal regions, is sustainable and reasonable?

Are there intelligent solutions to these questions that can accommodate inter-generational fairness and global responsibility? The principles of sustainability demand that we weigh economic values against the future life of the environment and develop concepts for sustainable solutions immediately. We need to understand how the ocean functions as a valuable ecosystem. We have to acknowledge our planet's limitations and work within them.

A sustainable use of the oceans is certainly possible! Steps in the right direction have already been taken: in the fall of 2015, the United Nations passed a new bill setting out sustainable development goals—for the first time with an explicit focus on our oceans, giving the problems visibility and political capital. A primary focus and objective of this book is to illuminate the biggest issues our oceans face, with the aim and profound hope that this encourages us to consider better solutions and a sustainable approach to managing our marine biospheres.

Prof Martin Visbeck
GEOMAR Helmholtz Centre
for Ocean Research in Kiel

Humanity...

We profit from the oceans and use them as a:

Food provider
Fish, algae and bivalves constitute the staples of many people's diets.

Poverty reducer
In many developing countries, fish provides the only affordable source of protein.

Energy and resource supplier
From petroleum to offshore wind farms.

Employer
Up to 12% of all employed people worldwide are dependent on the fishing industry.

Transportation route
Billions of goods are transported across the oceans annually.

Medication provider
Several medications are produced with substances extracted from the ocean.

Oasis of rest and recreation Beaches and coastal regions are popular recreational and vacation destinations.

How humanity threatens the oceans:

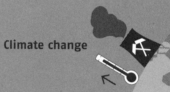

Climate change

Pollution

Industrialization

Overfishing

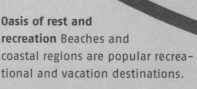

...and the sea

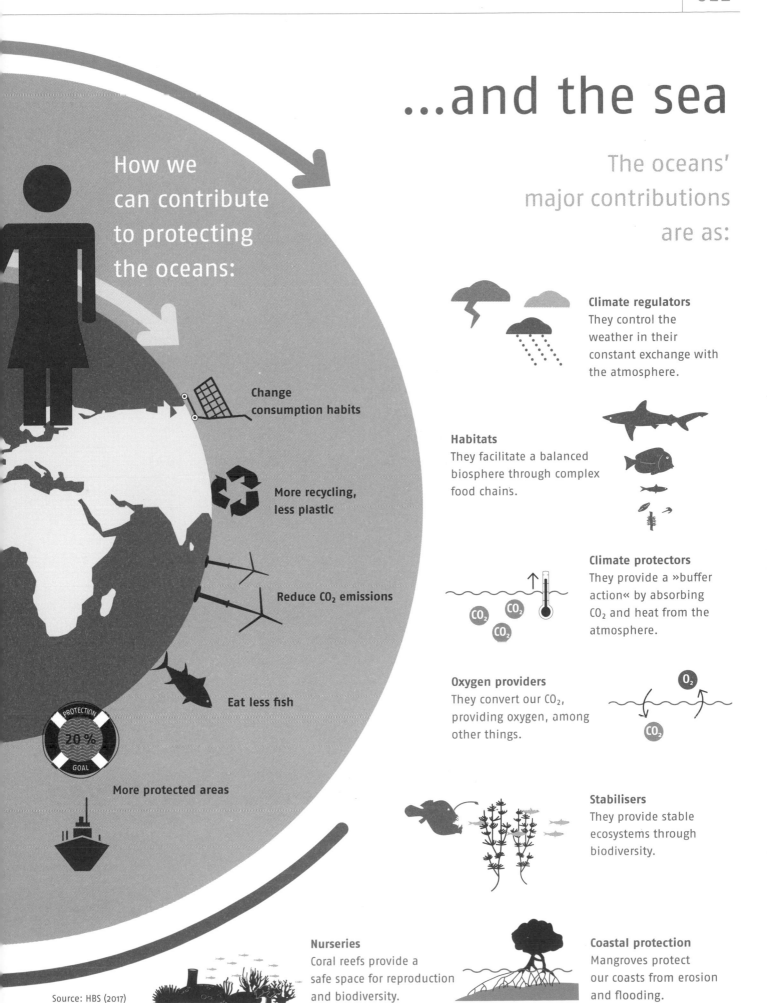

How we can contribute to protecting the oceans:

Change consumption habits

More recycling, less plastic

Reduce CO_2 emissions

Eat less fish

PROTECTION 70% GOAL

More protected areas

The oceans' major contributions are as:

Climate regulators
They control the weather in their constant exchange with the atmosphere.

Habitats
They facilitate a balanced biosphere through complex food chains.

Climate protectors
They provide a »buffer action« by absorbing CO_2 and heat from the atmosphere.

Oxygen providers
They convert our CO_2, providing oxygen, among other things.

Stabilisers
They provide stable ecosystems through biodiversity.

Nurseries
Coral reefs provide a safe space for reproduction and biodiversity.

Coastal protection
Mangroves protect our coasts from erosion and flooding.

Source: HBS (2017)

Causes → direct consequences → indirect consequences → approach to solutions

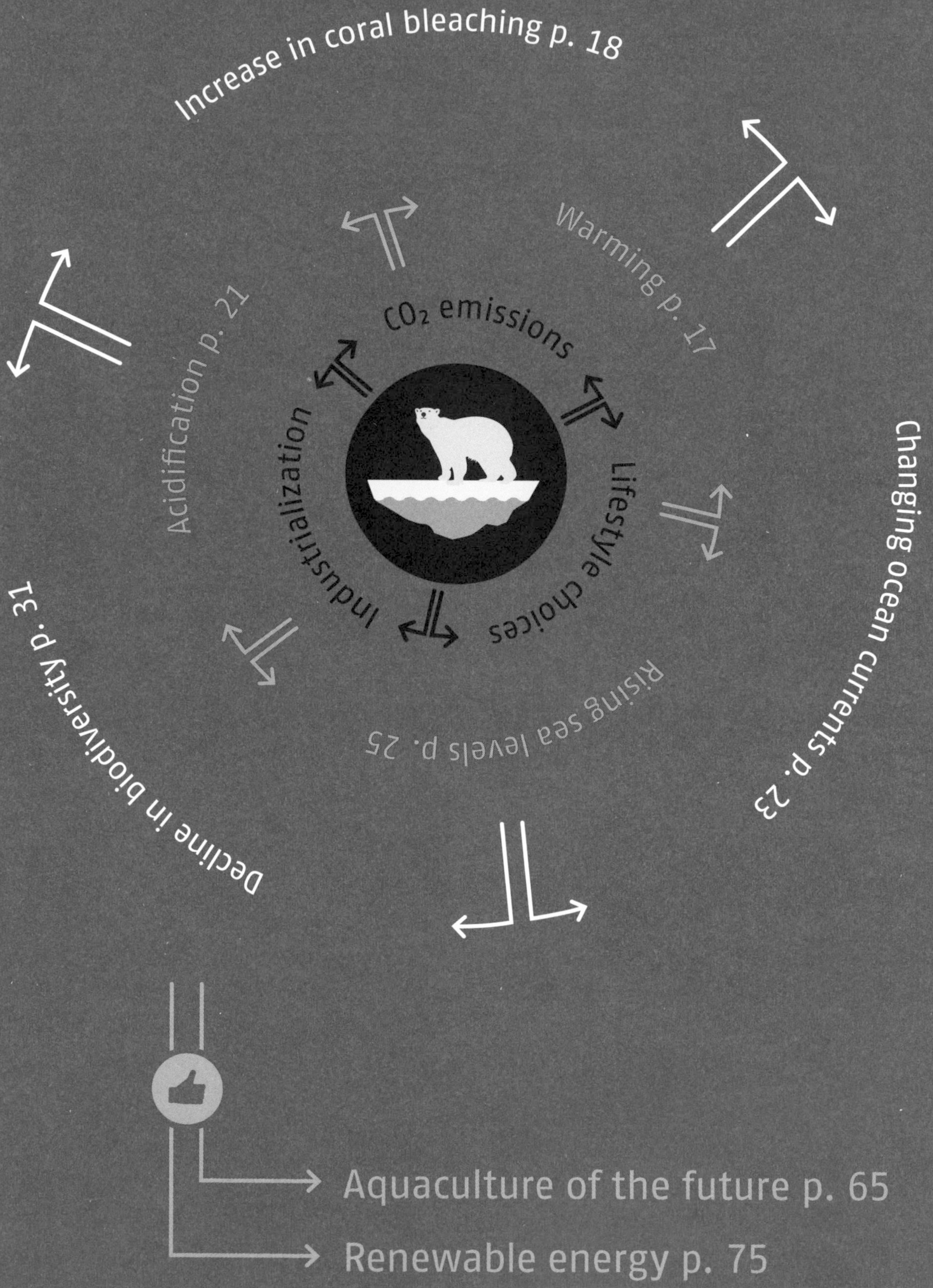
CO2 emissions
Lifestyle choices
Industrialization
Warming p. 17
Rising sea levels p. 25
Acidification p. 21
Increase in coral bleaching p. 18
Changing ocean currents p. 23
Decline in biodiversity p. 31
Aquaculture of the future p. 65
Renewable energy p. 75

Climate change

How does the climate work?

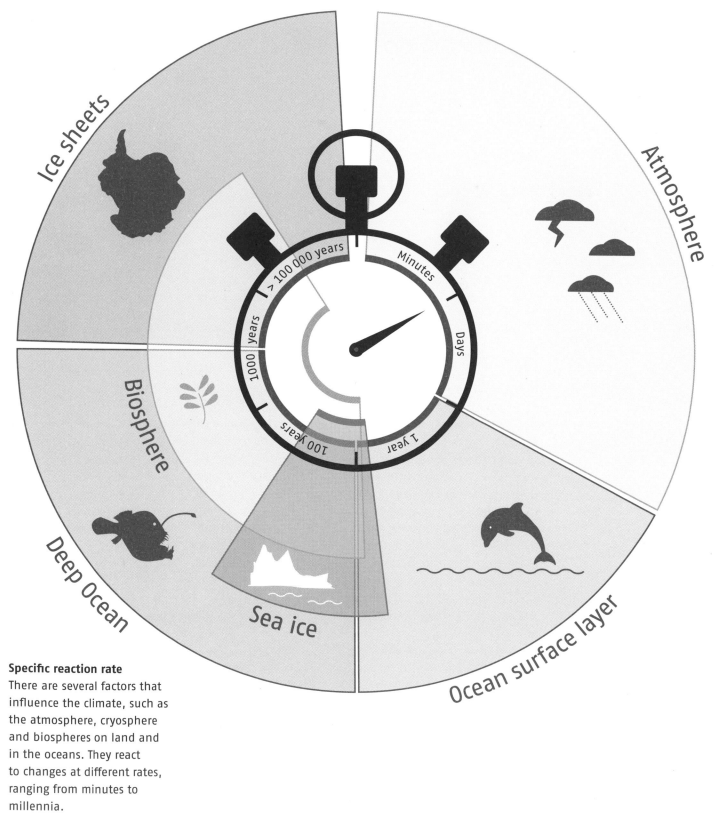

Specific reaction rate
There are several factors that influence the climate, such as the atmosphere, cryosphere and biospheres on land and in the oceans. They react to changes at different rates, ranging from minutes to millennia.

Sources: Jouzel et al. (2007), Maribus (2010), NASA (2015)

The history of global climate
Changes in the average
temperature and composition
of the earth's atmosphere
throughout the planet's history
can be scientifically followed
by analysing gas trapped in
bubbles in the arctic ice sheets.
The oxygen proportions allow us
to infer the earth's atmospheric
history for up to 800 000 years.

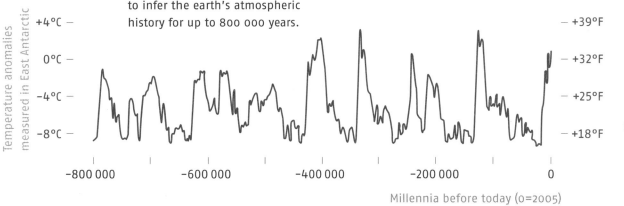

Millennia before today (0=2005)

Our planet has warmed up and cooled down more than once in its long history. Subtle changes in the earth's angle to the sun, the planet's surface, the atmosphere and fluctuations in the sun's intensity have always caused the climate to vary steadily. The greenhouse effect, for instance, is in fact an important climate factor for our survival. If sunlight entering the earth's atmosphere were not converted into warmth after being reflected off the earth's surface and partially absorbed by the atmosphere, we would be experiencing sub-zero temperatures.

Since the beginnings of industrialization in the 19th century, however, our emissions of CO_2 and other trace gases have contributed to an additional warming of the planet's surface. The more man-made CO_2 enters the atmosphere, the more thermal radiation remains trapped, leading to a more serious greenhouse situation. Scientists have been able to reconstruct the last 800 000 years of anomalies in the earth's temperature by analysing ice cores drilled in the Antarctic. This data,

as well as other climate archives, show us that the current change to the climate is occurring much faster than instances of global warming in the past.

This climate change has grave repercussions for the oceans. Because the surface of the sea is relatively dark, it absorbs considerable amounts of heat. Its slow ocean currents transport huge amounts of heat and CO_2. The sudden and extreme influx of CO_2 to the oceans is disturbing because the resulting acidification causes irreparable damage to ecosystems, ocean dwellers and coral reefs.

The ocean's climate responds relatively slowly to the greenhouse effect: the oceanic surface layer, stirred up by the wind, can react within months or years. It can take the deep sea centuries or even millennia to change. The ice sheets are the slowest, taking several hundreds and even thousands of years to show signs of change. Once they have begun, such far-reaching processes cannot be reversed by humankind. This is why global CO_2 emissions must be reduced as quickly as possible.

The anomalies of ocean heat

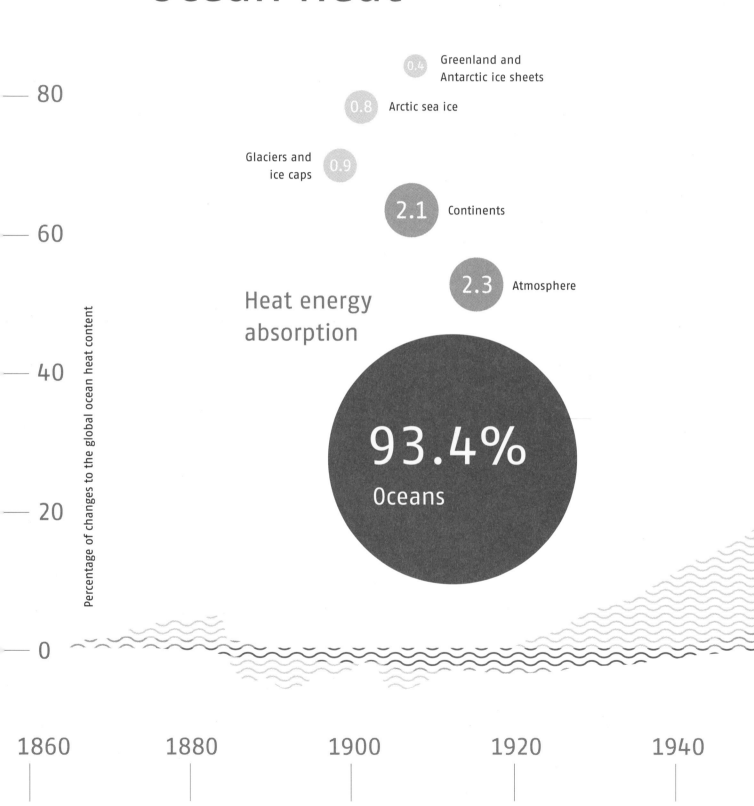

100%

80

60

40

20

0

Percentage of changes to the global ocean heat content

0.4 Greenland and Antarctic ice sheets

0.8 Arctic sea ice

Glaciers and ice caps 0.9

2.1 Continents

2.3 Atmosphere

Heat energy absorption

93.4%
Oceans

1860   1880   1900   1920   1940

Measured
ocean depth   〜 0–700m (0–2300ft)   〜 700–2000m (2300–6600ft)   〜 2000m (6600ft) to the ocean floor

2015 – in only 18 years
the thermal energy
stored by the oceans
has risen by
another 50%.

In 1997 a 50% increase
in thermal energy was
found to be stored in
the ocean's surface layer,
in comparison to
pre-industrial times.

The ocean has the greatest thermal
storage capacity on earth. While the
atmosphere just keeps getting hotter
and hotter, the ocean slows down our
man-made rise in temperature levels
considerably. The water gets warmer and
thus expands, which contributes to rising sea levels. At first, the heat is mostly
stored close to the surface, but then it
later moves down into the deep sea. In
this process heat is not only stored, but
also released: most of the heat is bound
close to the Equator. Surface currents
such as the Gulf Stream then transport
this warmth up north, where parts of
the heat are released into the atmosphere.

Between 1997 and 2015 the temperature absorption of the ocean's surface
layer has doubled, the medium depths
have experienced an increase of 35%,
while global warming has accelerated
significantly in parallel.

Alongside land-based biospheres, the
ocean is currently our strongest climate
fighting agent, but how much more heat
can the ocean absorb?

1960   1980   2000   2020   years

Sources: EPA (2014), Gleckler et al. (2016), IPCC (2013)

Consequences of warming

1 The ocean temperature rises

The Sea Surface Temperature (SST) tends to rise. The ocean is about .4°C(.7°F) warmer compared to the years between 1961 and 1990, as three different scientific models prove.

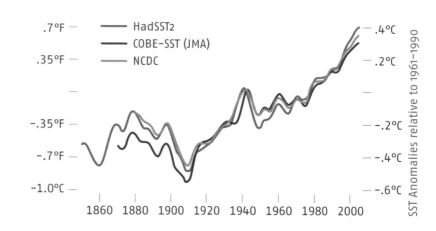

.7°F —   —— HadSST2   — .4°C
.35°F —   —— COBE–SST (JMA)   — .2°C
—   —— NCDC
−.35°F —   — −.2°C
−.7°F —   — −.4°C
−1.0°C —   — −.6°C

1860 1880 1900 1920 1940 1960 1980 2000

SST Anomalies relative to 1961–1990

2 Increasing numbers of coral reefs bleach and die off

The El Niño phenomenon, which occurs approximately every four years and during which the eastern equatorial Pacific region shows an unusually strong increase in warmth, causes mass coral mortality. Global warming, and the resulting warming up of the oceans, carries the consequence that the El Niño phenomenon tends to be stronger and last longer. The shorter the warming lasts, the higher the chances that the corals survive. The longest coral bleaching event so far began in October 2015 and lasted until May 2016. 93% of Australia's Great Barrier Reef, the earth's largest coral reef, was affected by this. In the northern parts of the reef, 50% of the bleached corals died.

↓

Corals engage in a symbiosis with certain algae, the zooxanthellae, which are indispensable to life. They are fed by the algae and gain their colour through them.

At a 1°C (2°F) rise in temperature, the algae go into a state of shock and produce toxins instead of sugars. The coral then rejects its partners and loses its colour.

The corals starve as a result of this. After their death, a dangerous process of algae and sponge coverage begins, making the return of zooxanthellae virtually impossible.

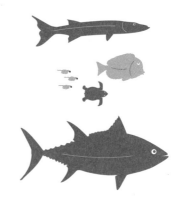

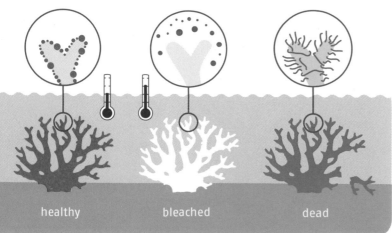

healthy   bleached   dead

→ **25%** of the ocean's inhabitants are directly dependent on coral reefs

③ Many marine creatures change their behaviour

When the waters are warmer than usual in the spring, many fish lay their eggs early. The food sources the larvae are used to may not be available yet at this point, since plankton are highly dependent on sunlight and the seasons. The consequence: larvae starve and the fish population diminishes.

Natural signs, such as the intensification of sunlight in spring and rising water temperatures in the summer, can trigger fishes to change their feeding and mating habits. Climate change can thus warp the natural behaviour of marine creatures, throwing ecosystems out of balance.

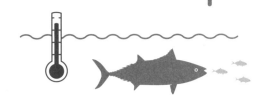

Invasive species spread out and alter ecosystems ④

Herbivorous tropical fish can do great damage. Masked rabbit fish, for example, which moved into the warming Mediterranean waters through the Suez canal, have been eating the native kelp and algae forests to destruction. This changes not only the environment, but also the behaviour of native fish.

−60%
plant biomass

Sources: ARC (2016), IPCC (2014), Neuheimer et al. (2015), Vergers et al. (2014), XL Catlin (2016)

Rising acidity

For 650 000 years, CO_2 levels in the atmosphere oscillated below 300 ppm. Then came the industrial revolution.

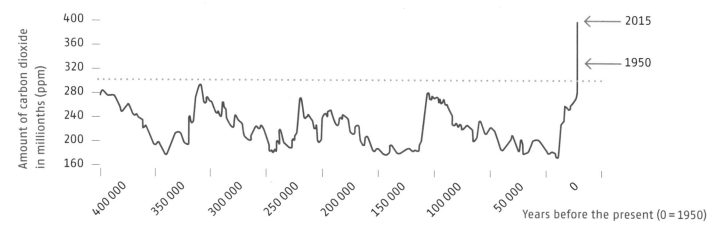

Since the age of industrialization, humanity has been burning massive amounts of fossil fuels and engaging in unprecedented scales of deforestation, causing the steady rise of carbon dioxide levels in the atmosphere and, consequently, in the ocean as well. Since then, the levels of CO_2 in the ocean have been increasing faster than in the previous 60 million years. The ocean's pH value has gone from 8.2 to 8.1 since 1950, meaning that the ocean's acidity is approximately 30% higher. It is estimated that if the rate of CO_2 emissions continues at the current level, it would cause a further increase of 140% by 2100. Ocean water is generally alkaline and only acidifies when it absorbs carbon dioxide and partially bonds to create carbonic acid. Marine plants such as algae take the carbon which has been dissolved in the water and metabolise it into sugars and starches through photosynthesis. Higher CO_2 levels also help jellyfish grow faster. But a continued drop in the ocean's pH balance would harm coral reefs and some invertebrate species, whose vital lime formation processes become impaired. We can only guess at how the entire ocean ecosystem would change with this continued drop in its pH levels, because, so far, there have not been sufficient long-term studies to provide us with data.

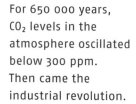

Carbon dioxide (CO_2)
Water (H_2O)
Carbonat ions (CO_3^{2-})
Bicarbonate ($2HCO_3^{-}$)

Sources: IGBP, IOC, SCOR (2013), Maribus (2010), CC (2010), NOAA (2016)

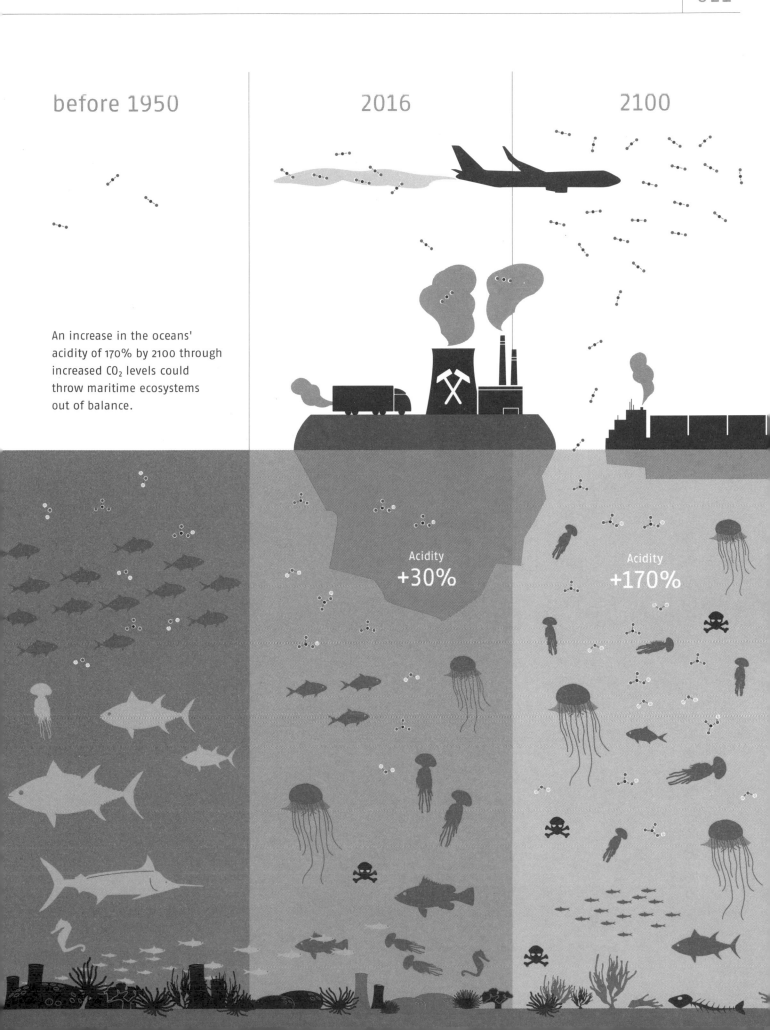

before 1950

2016

2100

An increase in the oceans' acidity of 170% by 2100 through increased CO_2 levels could throw maritime ecosystems out of balance.

Acidity +30%

Acidity +170%

Ocean currents in turmoil

Greenland's ice sheets are melting more rapidly than expected. Summer melt waters flow to the oceans in enormous rivers below the ice. Glaciers are calving and icebergs are melting directly into the ocean. The result is an acceleration in the rising of sea levels, while the salt levels in the northern seas drop.

Higher precipitation in the polar regions, caused by climate change, reduces the ocean's salt content, thus also lowering its surface density.

- ● Warm salt water
- ○ Cold salt water
- ● Cold fresh water

100m (330ft)

Ice sheets are made of fresh water. It is lighter than the denser salt water of the oceans. The more the ice sheets melt, causing fresh water to mix with salt water, the slower the rate of descent becomes.

The surface water coming from the south, once warm, cools down near Greenland in the convection area. Through its higher density (salt content) it sinks into the depths faster. This phenomenon acts like a giant circulation pump.

3000m (9900 ft)

Salty water is heavier and thus sinks faster than the fresh water run-off from melting glaciers.

25%
less convection of the oceans until 2100

Sources: Maribus (2010), NASA (2012), Rahmstorf (2015)

Thermohaline Circulation

Convection areas

...also known as the "conveyor" belt, is a complex network of surface, deep water and bottom currents, powered by differences in temperature and salt content, as well as winds. Thermohaline circulation is responsible for the Gulf Stream—the great North Atlantic current that flows towards Iceland.

····· Surface current

····· Deep water current

····· Bottom current

→ Direction of flow

Sinking waters

Ascending waters

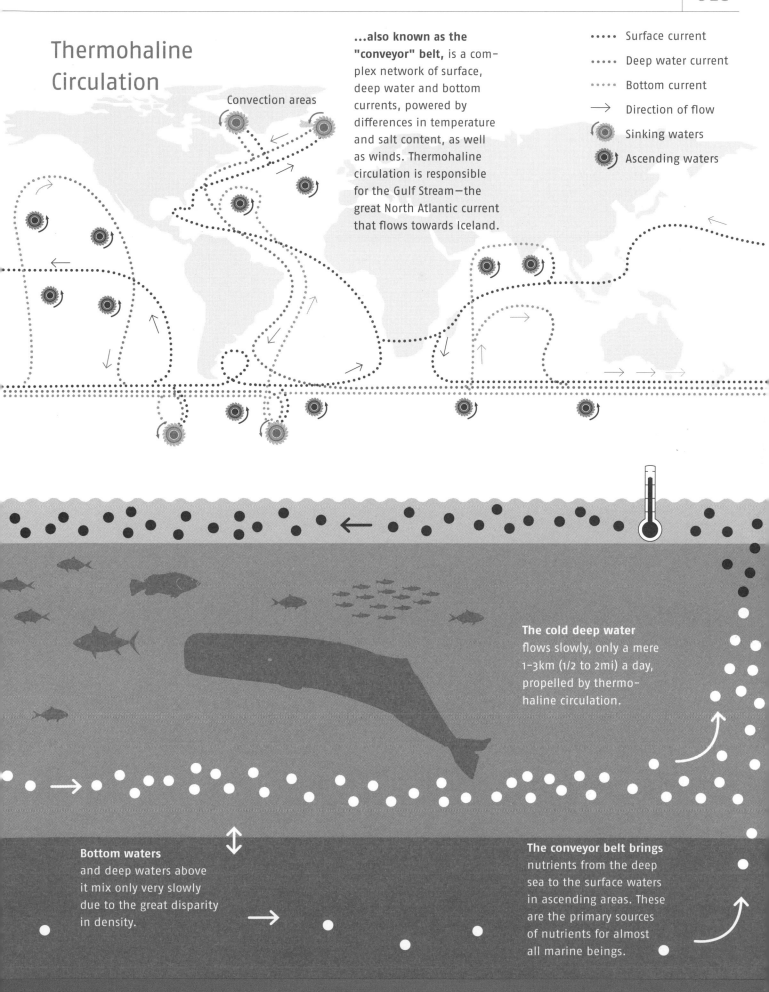

The cold deep water flows slowly, only a mere 1–3km (1/2 to 2mi) a day, propelled by thermohaline circulation.

Bottom waters and deep waters above it mix only very slowly due to the great disparity in density.

The conveyor belt brings nutrients from the deep sea to the surface waters in ascending areas. These are the primary sources of nutrients for almost all marine beings.

Rising sea level

The sea level has risen approximately 125m (410ft) since the last ice age, largely due to ice melt. Additionally, the ocean has expanded because of a rise in the average temperature on earth. Glaciers and ice sheets are melting with alarming speed, and the consequent release of fresh water flows through rivers into the sea.

The 12 000 year melting process, which began 21 000 years ago at the height of the last ice age, and has stagnated for 6 000 years, has begun with renewed and accelerated force through man-made climate change. For years, industrialised nations like The Netherlands have been gearing up for rising sea levels with expensive dikes and flood systems. People in poorer nations will be forced to flee inland. Continuing the global CO_2 emissions trend would cause an additional rise of 5m (16ft) in the next 300 years.

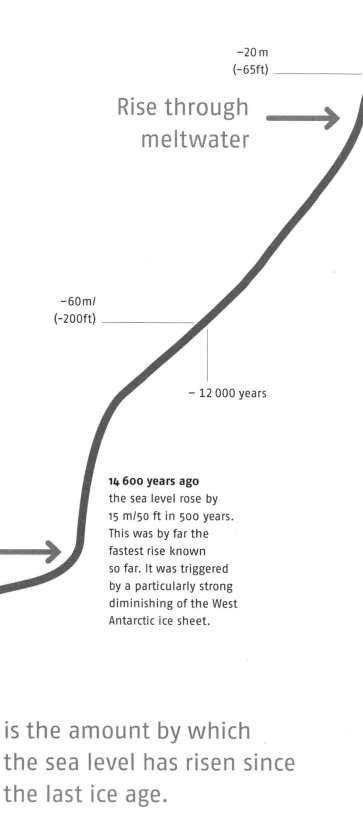

−20 m
(−65ft)

Rise through meltwater

−60m/
(−200ft)

− 12 000 years

14 600 years ago
the sea level rose by 15 m/50 ft in 500 years. This was by far the fastest rise known so far. It was triggered by a particularly strong diminishing of the West Antarctic ice sheet.

Rise through meltwater

−120m
(−400ft)

− 21 000 years

125m
(410ft)

is the amount by which the sea level has risen since the last ice age.

Sources: IPCC (2014), Maribus (2010), Pollard & deConto (2016), Vermeer & Rahmstorf (2009)

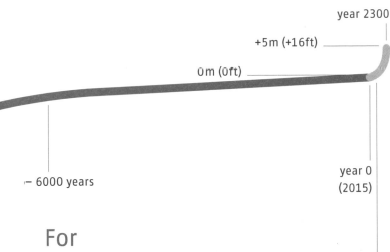

year 2300

+5m (+16ft)

0m (0ft)

6000 years

year 0
(2015)

year 2100

In
300 years
the ocean could rise
by another 5m (16ft).

For
6000 years
sea levels have stayed
nearly constant.

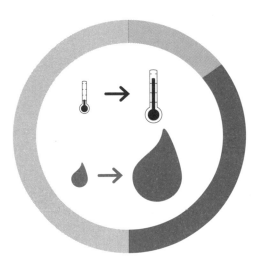

15–50%

is the amount
by which the
warming and
expansion of the
oceans contribute
to higher water
levels.

Latest (2016) prognosis
resulting from ice sheet
computer simulations

IPCC worst case
scenario

IPCC best case
scenario

180cm (71in)	
160cm (63in)	
140cm (55in)	
120cm (47in)	
100cm (39in)	
80cm (32in)	
60cm (24in)	
40cm (16in)	
0cm(in)	

Prognosis of the rising sea level
(up until 2100)

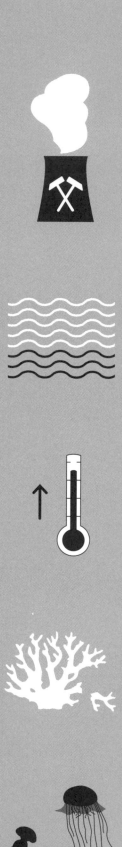

"By increasing
CO_2 emissions, mankind
is changing the planet's climate
in an unprecedented way.
The ocean of the future
will be warmer and more acidic,
to the detriment of coral reefs,
the marine food chain
and biodiversity.
The time for negotiation is over.
The time for action
is overdue."

Prof Axel Timmermann,
Pusan National University, Korea

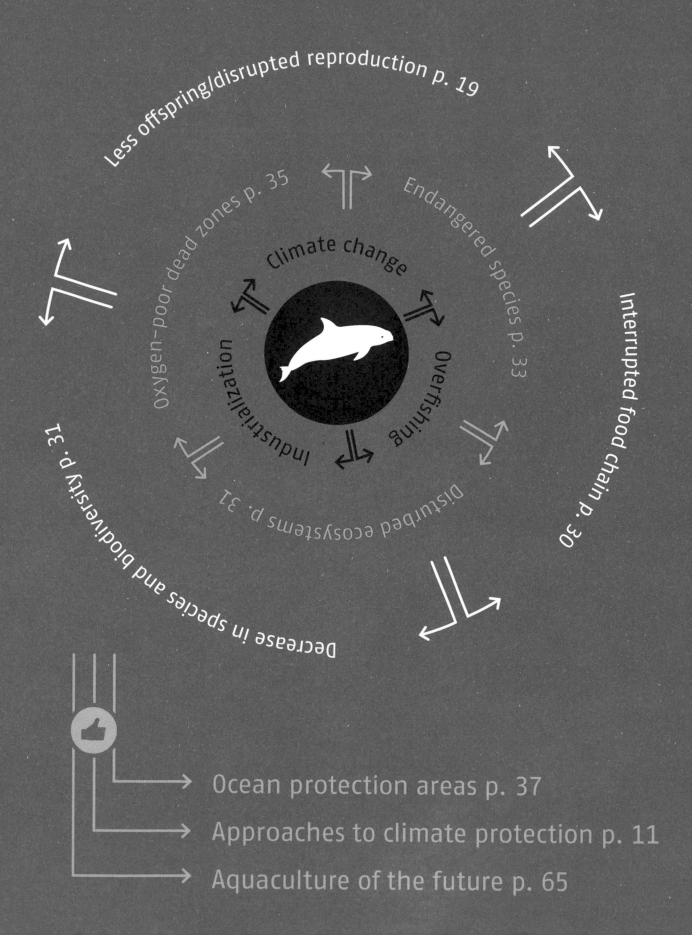

→ Causes → direct consequences → indirect consequences → approach to solutions

Less offspring/disrupted reproduction p. 19

Endangered species p. 33

Oxygen-poor dead zones p. 35

Climate change

Overfishing

Industrialization

Disturbed ecosystems p. 31

Decrease in species and biodiversity p. 31

Interrupted food chain p. 30

Ocean protection areas p. 37

Approaches to climate protection p. 11

Aquaculture of the future p. 65

Loss
of biological
diversity

Marine Biodiversity

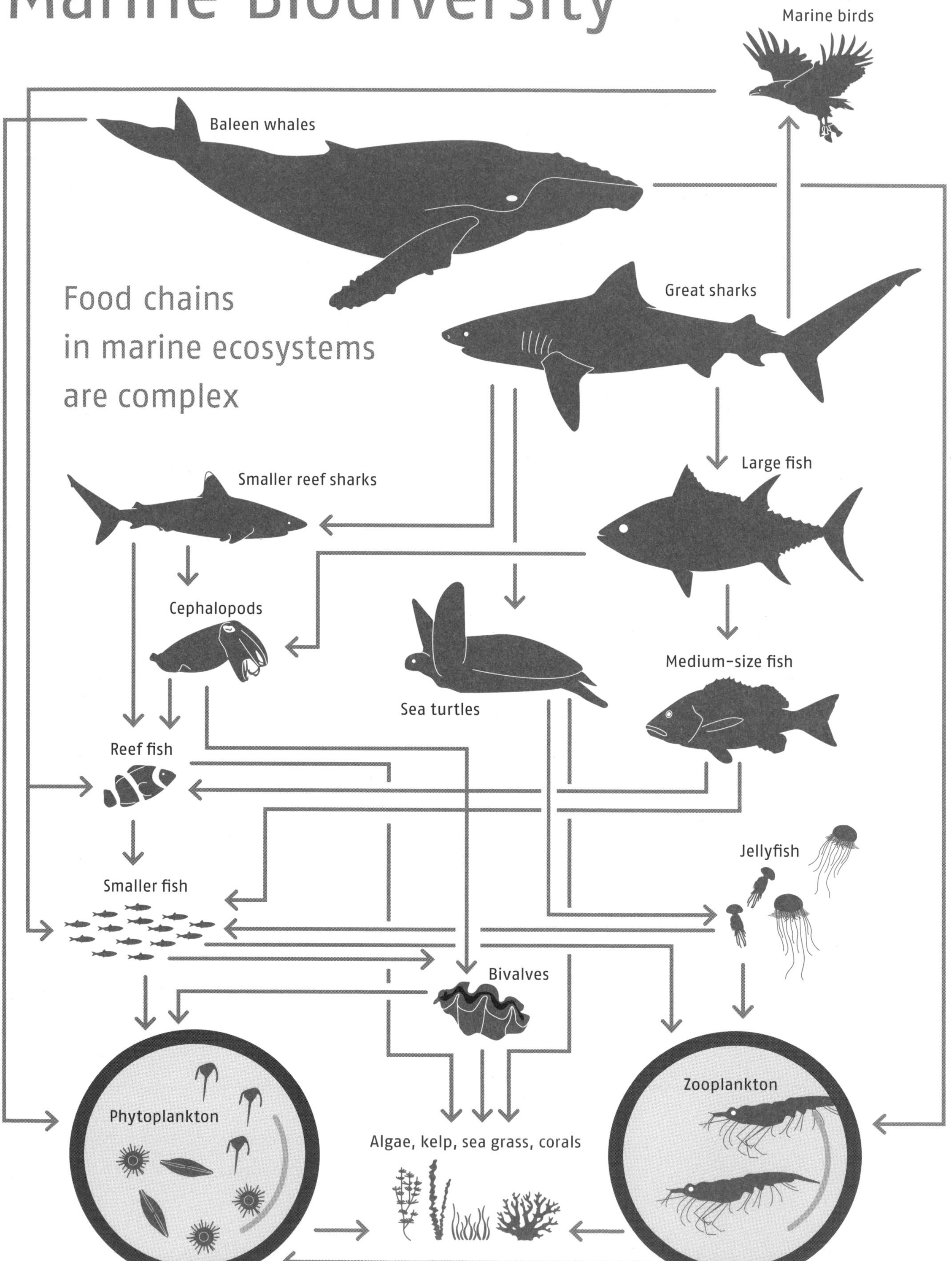

Marine birds

Baleen whales

Great sharks

Food chains
in marine ecosystems
are complex

Smaller reef sharks

Large fish

Cephalopods

Sea turtles

Medium-size fish

Reef fish

Jellyfish

Smaller fish

Bivalves

Phytoplankton

Algae, kelp, sea grass, corals

Zooplankton

Sources: Mittermeier et al. (2011), Maribus (2010), William et al. (2016), Poulsen et al. (2016), Kieneke et al. (2015)

On average, three new species are discovered worldwide every day

Countless numbers of animal and plant species inhabit our oceans. Every day new members of this vast ecosystem are discovered. Every creature in the ocean, be it shark or plankton, plays its own unique role in the ecosystem. Decreases or changes in any single component can have a negative impact on the activity of the entire ecosystem. This is why the rapid loss of biodiversity is such a concern. Since the dawn of the industrial age, certain areas have experienced a decrease in biodiversity of 65 to 90%. The cause for this disturbing trend is humanity's destruction of entire habitats. Demersal trawls are dragged across the ocean floor, coastal wetlands are destroyed through over-fertilisation and development, and plastic is littered all over the oceans. The consequences are disastrous: as species become extinct, the ecosystem's ability to adapt and produce is weakened.

Gastrotrich
Discovered: 2015
Size: 450 µm (.02in)
Habitat: sediment

Mirrorbellies
(glows in the dark)
Discovered: 2016
Size: 6.5 cm (2.5in)
Habitat: deep sea

Brianne's groppo
Discovered: 2016
Size: 9 cm (3.5in)
Habitat: reefs

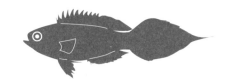

Intensity of biodiversity

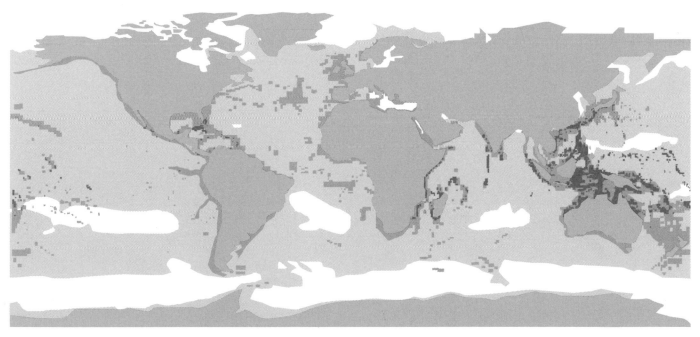

Biodiversity ■ very high (3364–8290*)   ■ high (554–3363)   ■ medium (92–553)   ☐ low (1–91)

* number of species per 0.5 degrees latitude and longitude

On the Red List
(due to overfishing and by–catch)

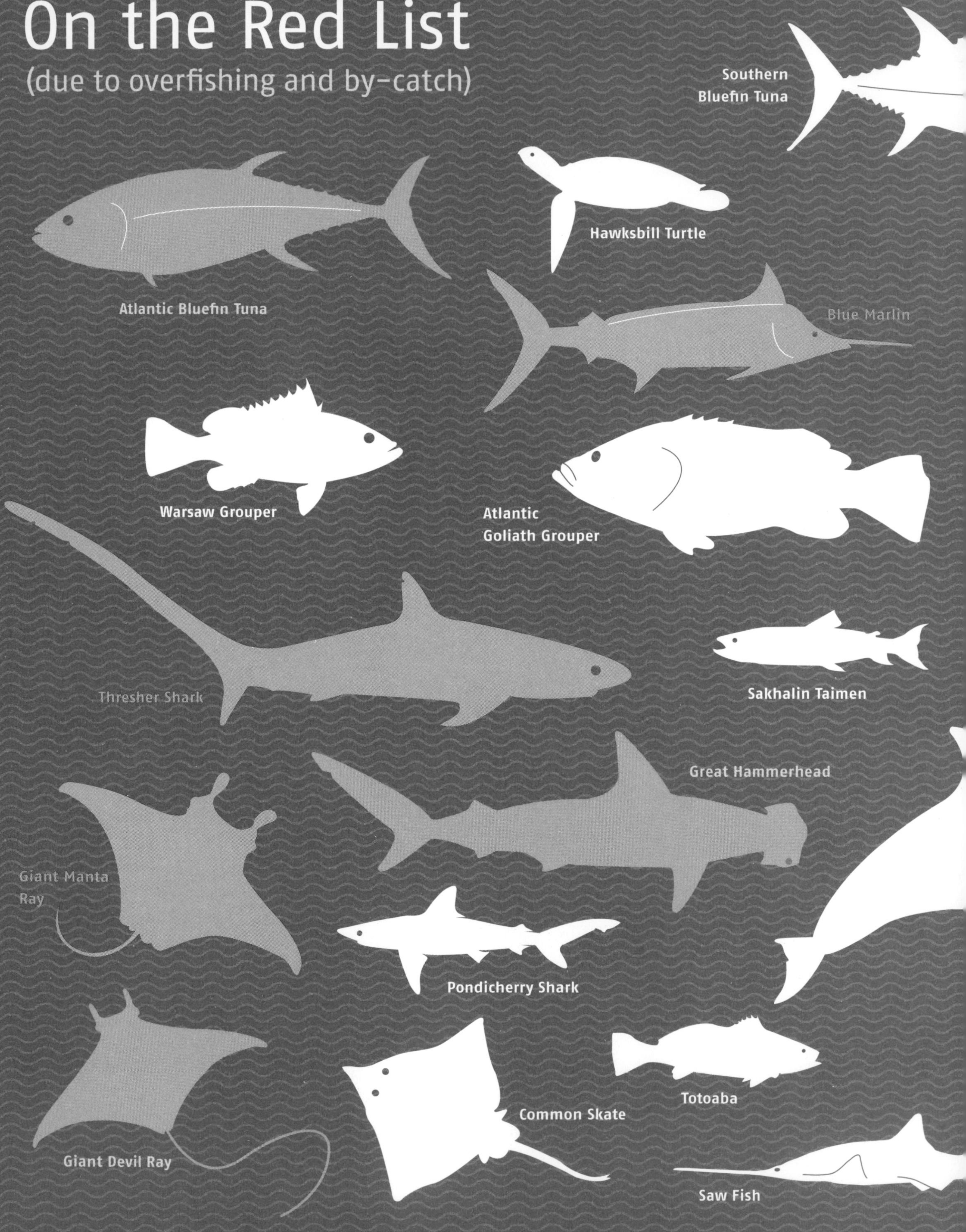

Southern
Bluefin Tuna

Hawksbill Turtle

Atlantic Bluefin Tuna

Blue Marlin

Warsaw Grouper

Atlantic
Goliath Grouper

Thresher Shark

Sakhalin Taimen

Great Hammerhead

Giant Manta
Ray

Pondicherry Shark

Totoaba

Common Skate

Giant Devil Ray

Saw Fish

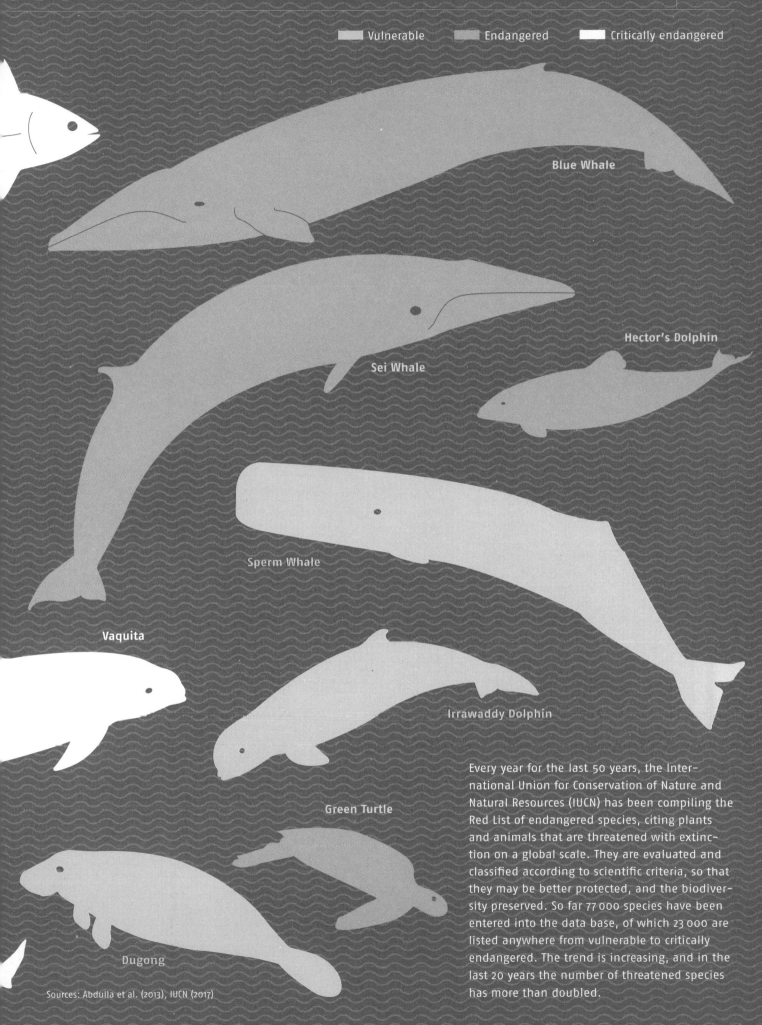

Vulnerable · Endangered · Critically endangered

Blue Whale

Sei Whale

Hector's Dolphin

Sperm Whale

Vaquita

Irrawaddy Dolphin

Green Turtle

Dugong

Every year for the last 50 years, the International Union for Conservation of Nature and
Natural Resources (IUCN) has been compiling the
Red List of endangered species, citing plants
and animals that are threatened with extinction on a global scale. They are evaluated and
classified according to scientific criteria, so that
they may be better protected, and the biodiversity preserved. So far 77 000 species have been
entered into the data base, of which 23 000 are
listed anywhere from vulnerable to critically
endangered. The trend is increasing, and in the
last 20 years the number of threatened species
has more than doubled.

Sources: Abdulla et al. (2013), IUCN (2017)

Oxygen-poor dead zones

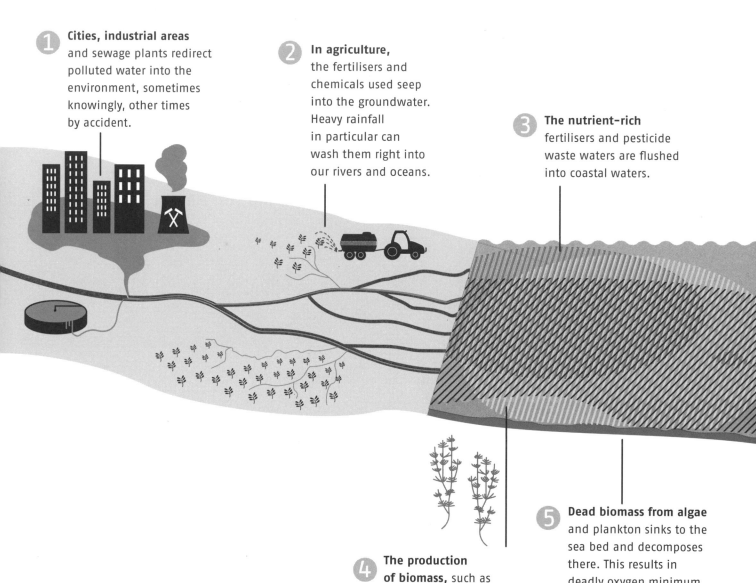

1 **Cities, industrial areas** and sewage plants redirect polluted water into the environment, sometimes knowingly, other times by accident.

2 **In agriculture,** the fertilisers and chemicals used seep into the groundwater. Heavy rainfall in particular can wash them right into our rivers and oceans.

3 **The nutrient-rich** fertilisers and pesticide waste waters are flushed into coastal waters.

4 **The production of biomass,** such as algae, increases in coastal waters due to the increased nutrients. The algae grow near the surface and thus slowly darken the deeper ocean layers, where plants die, starved of oxygen and light.

5 **Dead biomass from algae** and plankton sinks to the sea bed and decomposes there. This results in deadly oxygen minimum zones (OMZ), which expand and connect to other OMZs in the open ocean.

Eutrophication can alter entire coastal regions: the enormous increase of nutrients near rivers, particularly through agricultural waste waters, causes a disproportionate influx of phytoplankton and plant growth, leading in turn to more dead biomass on the sea bed. Bacteria decompose the dead plants, drawing oxygen from the water in the process. Fish that cannot adapt migrate away, most organisms living at the bottom simply die off, meadows of sea weed disappear, and what remains are resistant species such as jellyfish and certain algae.

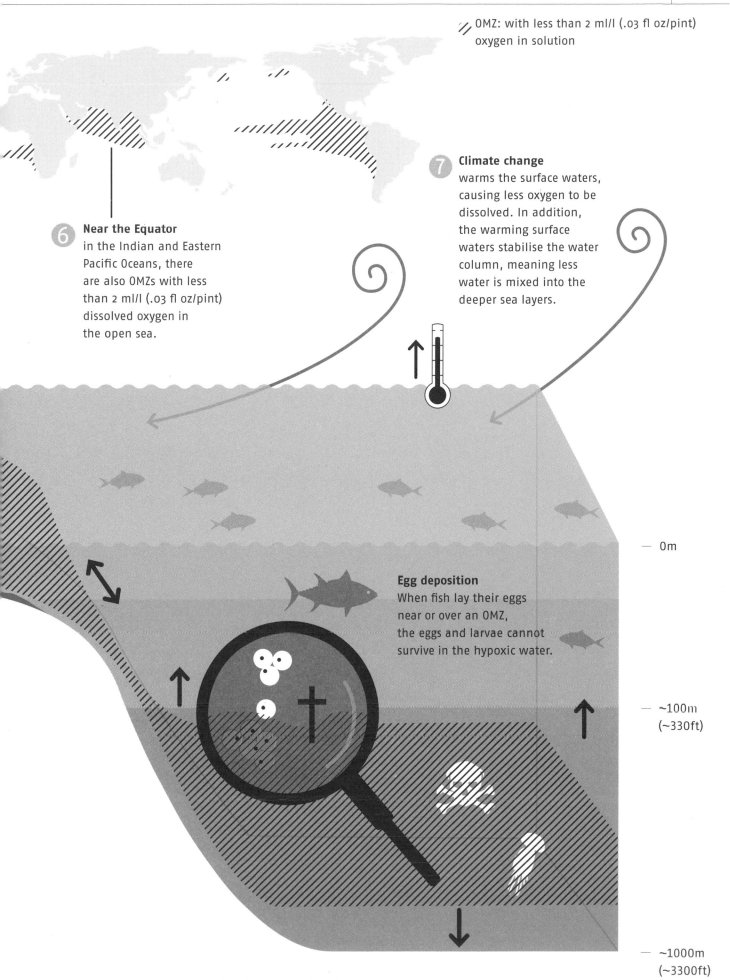

OMZ: with less than 2 ml/l (.03 fl oz/pint) oxygen in solution

7 Climate change warms the surface waters, causing less oxygen to be dissolved. In addition, the warming surface waters stabilise the water column, meaning less water is mixed into the deeper sea layers.

6 Near the Equator in the Indian and Eastern Pacific Oceans, there are also OMZs with less than 2 ml/l (.03 fl oz/pint) dissolved oxygen in the open sea.

Egg deposition When fish lay their eggs near or over an OMZ, the eggs and larvae cannot survive in the hypoxic water.

— 0m

— ~100m (~330ft)

— ~1000m (~3300ft)

Sources: Maribus (2010), Stramma et al. (2010), NODC/NOAA (2005)

Growing marine reserves

To ensure a sustainable future for humans and our planet, an increase in natural reserves on land and in the sea is indispensable. Protected zones preserve biodiversity and thus contribute to a healthy ecosystem, which in turn is better equipped to handle human interference and the problems created through climate change.

These protected areas also play a key role in the preservation of fish stocks and sustainable fishing practices.

At the moment (status at the end of 2016) there are over 14 600 marine protected areas (MPAs) globally spanning close to 15 million square kilometres (5.8 mln mi²). That is equivalent to 4% of the entire ocean expanse and 10.2% of coastal and marine areas under national jurisdiction. In national territorial waters, reserves have been growing by 1.8% annually since 2014, which translates into 2.6 million square kilometres. In areas beyond national jurisdiction, which constitute 58% of the total, only 0.25% are under protection, and, unfortunately, show no growth trend.

The trailblazers of ocean conservation are Australia, New Caledonia, South Georgia and the Southern Sandwich Islands.

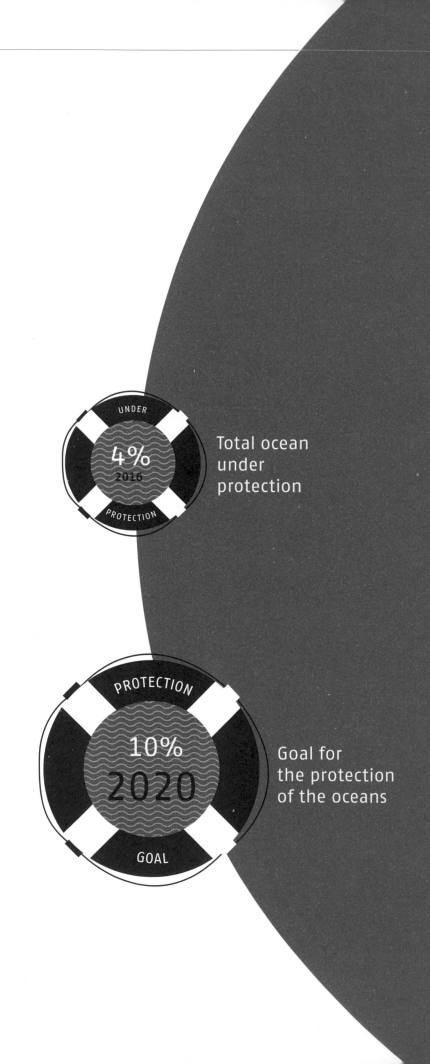

UNDER
4%
2016
PROTECTION

Total ocean under protection

PROTECTION
10%
2020
GOAL

Goal for the protection of the oceans

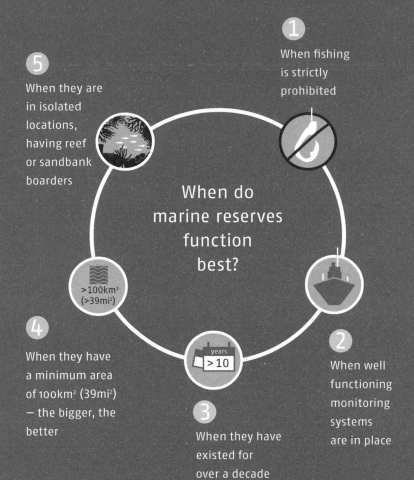

1 When fishing is strictly prohibited

5 When they are in isolated locations, having reef or sandbank boarders

When do marine reserves function best?

4 When they have a minimum area of 100km² (39mi²) – the bigger, the better

3 When they have existed for over a decade

2 When well functioning monitoring systems are in place

In a recent study of 124 different marine reserves in 29 countries, it was found that fish and other sea creatures were, on average, more numerous, and that the bio-diversity was generally richer, in these protected areas.

● Marine protected area (MPA) with fishing prohibition   ∘ɪ//ɪ/ MPA with fishing restrictions

Sources: AGDE (2016), UNEP–WCMC and IUCN (2016), Sciberras et al. (2015)

"Though the importance
of marine biodiversity has long
been unclear, scientists now
agree that it keeps marine ecosystems
efficient and stable and renders
habitats more resilient.
However, overfishing, climate change
and pollution are increasingly
destabilising the ocean's intricate
web of species."

Prof Hartmut Grassl,
Max Planck Institute Hamburg

→ Causes → direct consequences → indirect consequences → approach to solutions

Increased strain on endangered species p. 33
Interrupted food chains p. 31
Disturbance and stress of sensible ecosystems p. 19
High quantities of by-catch p. 59
Increased demand p. 43
Increased quantities of fishing p. 47
Fishing vessels
Fishing practices
Illegal fishing
Marine reserves p. 37
Aquaculture of the future p. 65

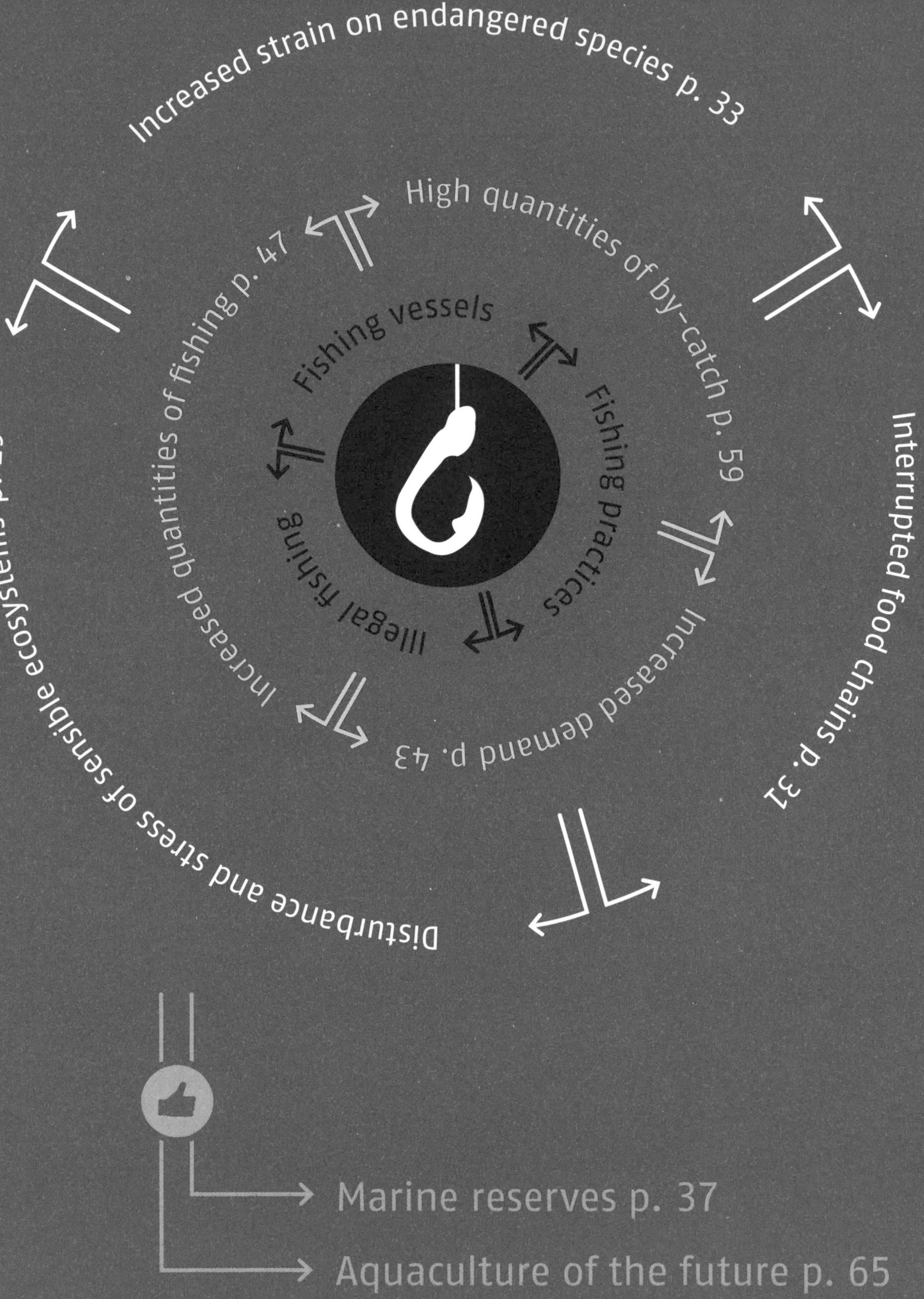

Overfishing

Facts about the fishing industry

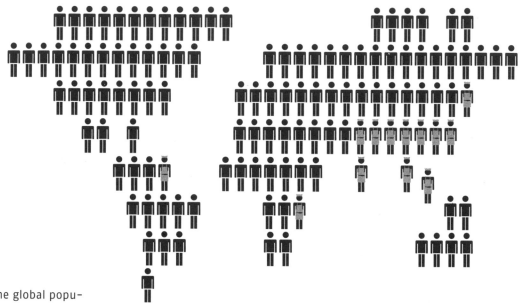

Livelihood

10 to 12% of the global population is dependent on fishing as a source of income. 84% of all people employed in fishing industries live in Asia, followed by 10% in Africa, and 4% in Latin America and the Caribbean respectively. An unknown number of people work on slave ships.

Global catch
in tons

Reconstructed gross catch ——
Upper and lower threshold ▨
Official catch ▨

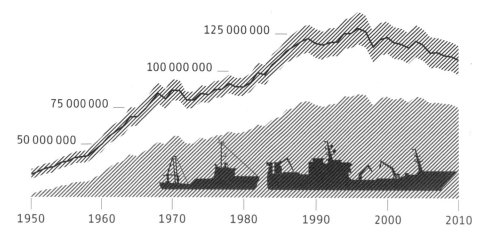

150 000 000 —

125 000 000 —

100 000 000 —

75 000 000 —

50 000 000 —

1950   1960   1970   1980   1990   2000   2010

The FAO's official catch figures were at their highest in 1996, at 86 million tons, slightly reducing thereafter. Once unofficial and illegal fishing and by-catch were included, however, scientists revised this number up to 130 million tons, with a sharper decline in later years.

Sources: FAO (2016), Pauly and Zeller (2016)

10kg (22lb)

1960

20kg (44lb)

2013

While fish consumption has remained steady and even fallen in some countries, it has been steadily growing in developing nations. The highest consumption of fish, however, occurs in industrial nations, with an average of 26.8kg (59lb) per person a year. The fish consumed there is mainly imported.

Globally over
1 billion
people are dependent on fish as their primary food source.

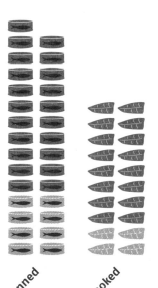

Fish processing
While fish is largely consumed fresh in the developing world, industrial nations buy their fish mostly frozen. Overall, most fish is caught and processed in developing nations.

Live, fresh or chilled

Frozen

Canned

Smoked

Non food purposes

Developing nations

Industrial nations

 1 million tons (live weight)

Intense levels of fishing

Fish stock is counted as overfished when the amount of fish caught exceeds the number replenished through natural reproduction and immigration. The fact that, despite improved fishing practices, longer fishing trips, and increased efforts on the part of the fishing industry, the catch quantity is still going down is indicative of this. According to scientific research and calculations, 30 to 55% of fish stocks are considered overfished or have collapsed. A fish stock counts as collapsed when it has declined disproportionately in just a few years, making any recovery highly unlikely. To make fishing sustainable, scientifically–based fishing quotas, particularly for intensely overfished species, must be established and enforced on a global scale.

Source: Watson et al. (2012)

Fishing fleet: overcapacity

The global fishing fleet is estimated at 4.7 million ships, with the potential to diminish what fish resources we have.

Super trawlers with fish processing facilities, 120–144m (395–475ft),
can be at sea for several months

Fish trawlers with fish processing facilities, 70–90m (230–295ft), at sea for 1–2 months

Fishing vessels, 25–45m (80–145ft),
at sea for approximately 1–4 weeks

Traditional fishing boats, 7–10m (23–33ft),
at sea for one day at most

| 0m (ft) | 50m (165ft) | 100m (330ft) | 140m (460ft) |

250 000 people   60 000kg (132 000lb) of fish ·

Maximum catch
per trip

7 000 000kg
(15 430 000lb)

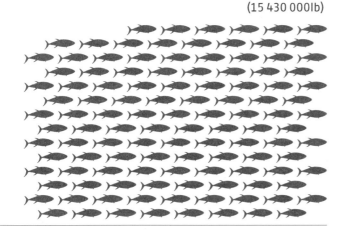

1 000 000 – 1 500 000kg
(2 200 000 – 3 300 000lb)

60 000kg
(132 000lb)

30 – 300kg
(65 – 650lb)

Persons employed in industrial scale fishing worldwide

500 000 people

Persons employed in traditional fishing practices worldwide

12 000 000 people

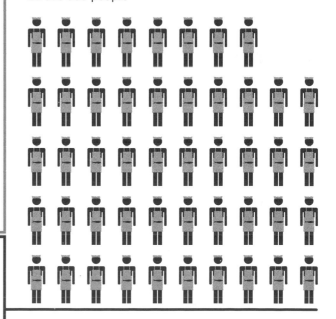

Sources: EU (2016), Greenpeace (2014), Shipping companies (2017)

Industrial fishing methods

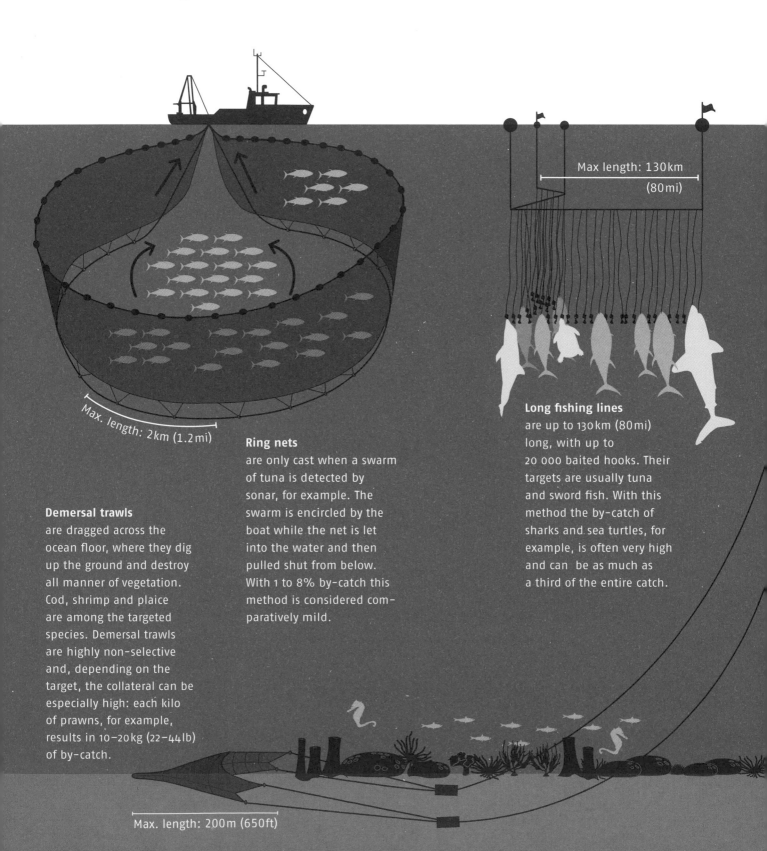

Max. length: 2km (1.2mi)

Max length: 130km (80mi)

Ring nets
are only cast when a swarm of tuna is detected by sonar, for example. The swarm is encircled by the boat while the net is let into the water and then pulled shut from below. With 1 to 8% by-catch this method is considered comparatively mild.

Long fishing lines
are up to 130km (80mi) long, with up to 20 000 baited hooks. Their targets are usually tuna and sword fish. With this method the by-catch of sharks and sea turtles, for example, is often very high and can be as much as a third of the entire catch.

Demersal trawls
are dragged across the ocean floor, where they dig up the ground and destroy all manner of vegetation. Cod, shrimp and plaice are among the targeted species. Demersal trawls are highly non-selective and, depending on the target, the collateral can be especially high: each kilo of prawns, for example, results in 10–20kg (22–44lb) of by-catch.

Max. length: 200m (650ft)

A percentage of by-catch is brought to land and is either put on the market or made into fishmeal. Unintentionally caught, injured or dead creatures are often thrown overboard. This discarding has meanwhile been made illegal in many countries.

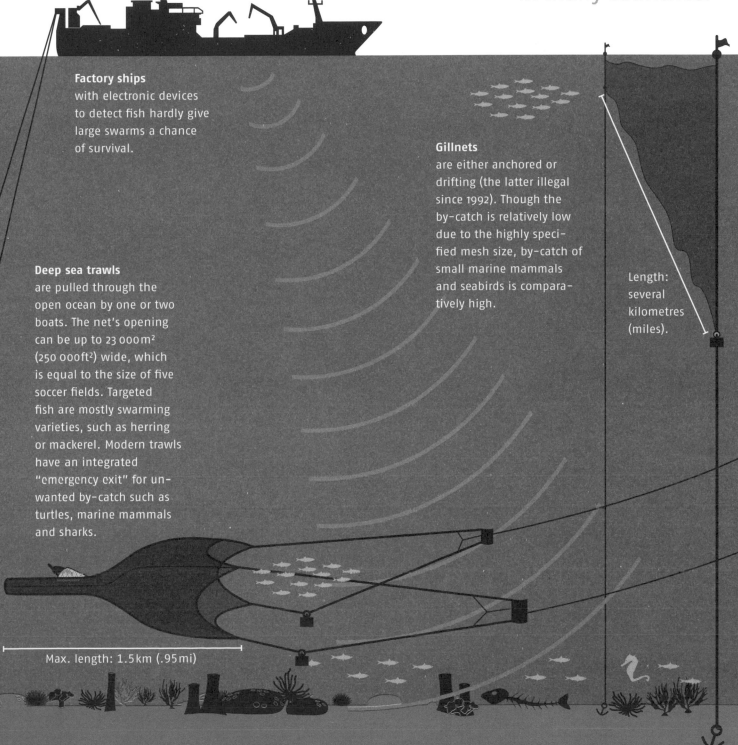

Factory ships
with electronic devices to detect fish hardly give large swarms a chance of survival.

Gillnets
are either anchored or drifting (the latter illegal since 1992). Though the by-catch is relatively low due to the highly speci-fied mesh size, by-catch of small marine mammals and seabirds is compara-tively high.

Deep sea trawls
are pulled through the open ocean by one or two boats. The net's opening can be up to 23 000 m² (250 000 ft²) wide, which is equal to the size of five soccer fields. Targeted fish are mostly swarming varieties, such as herring or mackerel. Modern trawls have an integrated "emergency exit" for un-wanted by-catch such as turtles, marine mammals and sharks.

Length: several kilometres (miles).

Max. length: 1.5 km (.95 mi)

Sources: ISSF (2017), Seafish (2015)

Traditional fishing

Traditional fishing vessels are often no more than 10m (33ft) long and open, as shown here in the example of Martinique's traditional fishing method.

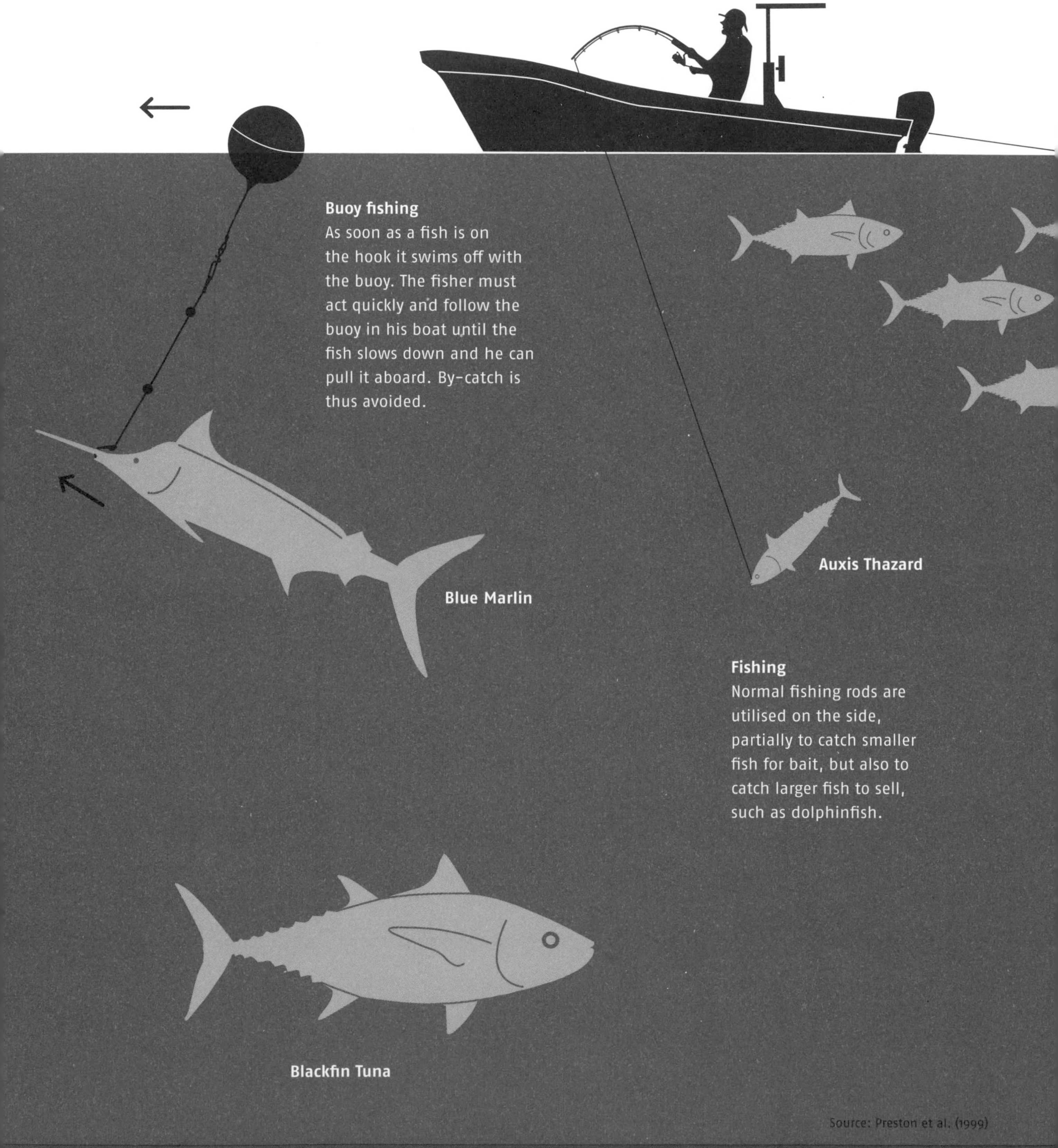

Buoy fishing
As soon as a fish is on the hook it swims off with the buoy. The fisher must act quickly and follow the buoy in his boat until the fish slows down and he can pull it aboard. By-catch is thus avoided.

Blue Marlin

Auxis Thazard

Fishing
Normal fishing rods are utilised on the side, partially to catch smaller fish for bait, but also to catch larger fish to sell, such as dolphinfish.

Blackfin Tuna

Source: Preston et al. (1999)

Surface trolling
A line of bait is dragged behind the boat, either on the surface or at depth, if additionally weighed down.

FAD: Fish Aggregating Device
A buoy that is anchored to the seabed has shimmering bands of fabric attached to a line. This "shelter" attracts smaller fish, which in turn attract larger fish. This method serves small scale fishermen well enough. When deployed by industrial fisheries, FADs cause high rates of by-catch of endangered species and young creatures.

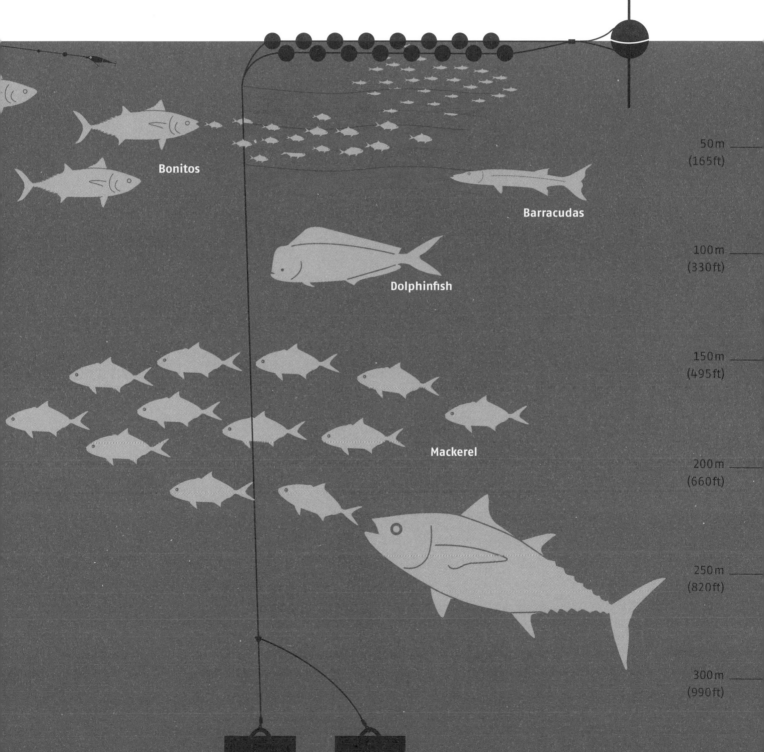

Bonitos

Barracudas

Dolphinfish

Mackerel

50m (165ft)

100m (330ft)

150m (495ft)

200m (660ft)

250m (820ft)

300m (990ft)

30% of tuna stocks are overfished

Tuna fish catch in 1950

0.4 million tons

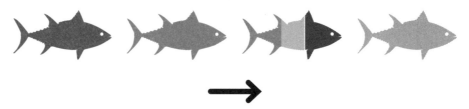

→

"According to the FAO, over 5 million tons of tuna were caught in 2014. 3 million of those tons were bonitos (skipjack), that are mostly canned, followed by yellowfin tuna (1.5 million tons), which is popular as steak or sushi, for example, bigeye tuna (0.40 million tons) and albacore (0.23 million tons). Catch of the highly endangered and high-priced Atlantic bluefin tuna grossed only 40 000 tons and constituted only 1% of the global tuna catch.

Not all tuna stocks are considered endangered, but approximately 30% are overfished, while only 17% of the population are considered to be in a middle or stable state (ISSF)."
Dr. Matthias Schaber,
Thünen Institute of Sea Fisheries

Sources: FAO (2016), ISSF (2017)

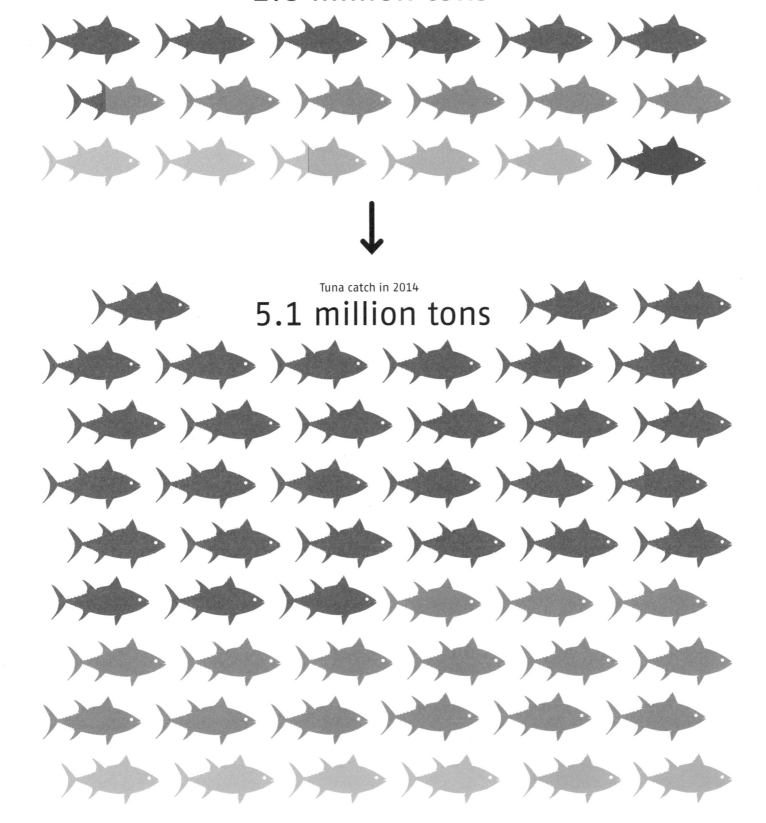

= Bonito/Skipjack   = Yellowfin   = Bigeye   = Albacore   = Bluefin

each approx. 0.1 million tons of tuna

Tuna catch in 1976

1.8 million tons

Tuna catch in 2014

5.1 million tons

Why sharks
are endangered

1

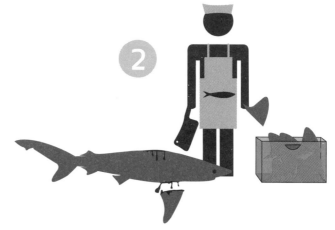

2

"Finning" is when shark
fins are removed from the
living creature aboard the
fishing boat before their
bodies are cast back into
the ocean. According
to the law, fishermen must
bring the entire shark back
to shore, but their bodies
are cumbersome, hard
to sell, often unpleasant
to eat, and take a long
time to process.

An estimated 67 to
273 million sharks are
caught annually, either
directly targeted or as
by-catch—mostly with
longline fishing—both legal
and illegal. The fins from
around 23 to 73 million
sharks are exported to Asia,
where demand for this
"delicacy" is very high.
The fins are often cut off
through a practice known
as "finning".

Evolved over 420 million years, sharks have
become the perfect predators inhabiting
a multitude of marine habitats. They play an
extremely important role as "reef police",
and are vital to maintaining for the balance
of the oceanic ecosystem. A quarter of the
over 450 known shark species are in danger
of extinction. Many have been reduced to
20% of their original populations. Sharks
are slow to mature and often produce few
offspring, which is why overfished populations take longer to recover.

Sources: Clarke et al. (2007), EC (2011), FAO (2014), IUCN (2003), WildAid (2014)

3 Still alive as they are thrown overboard, the mutilated creatures sink to the ocean floor, unable to move. Without motion they are unable to absorb oxygen through their gills, causing them to either suffocate, or perish as a result of their injuries.

4

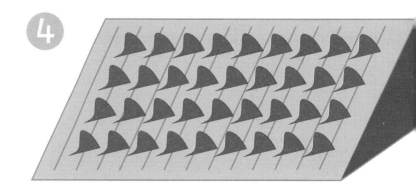

Every year, middle men dry an estimated 260 million shark fins illegally on their harbour rooftops or in their backyards.

5

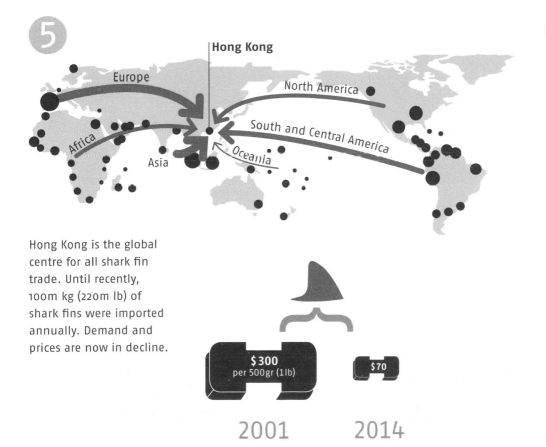

Hong Kong

Europe

North America

Africa

South and Central America

Asia

Oceania

Hong Kong is the global centre for all shark fin trade. Until recently, 100m kg (220m lb) of shark fins were imported annually. Demand and prices are now in decline.

$300 per 500gr (1lb)

$70

2001   2014

6

Shark fin soup is a traditional wedding soup in China. Educational campaigns work to remove this dish from the menus at top restaurants around the globe. This "delicacy" costs upwards of $90, but supposedly has no flavour of its own. Additionally, shark fin in tincture and powdered form is sold all over Asia as a potency supplement—the actual efficacy of which has never been proven.

Dolphin hunting in Taiji

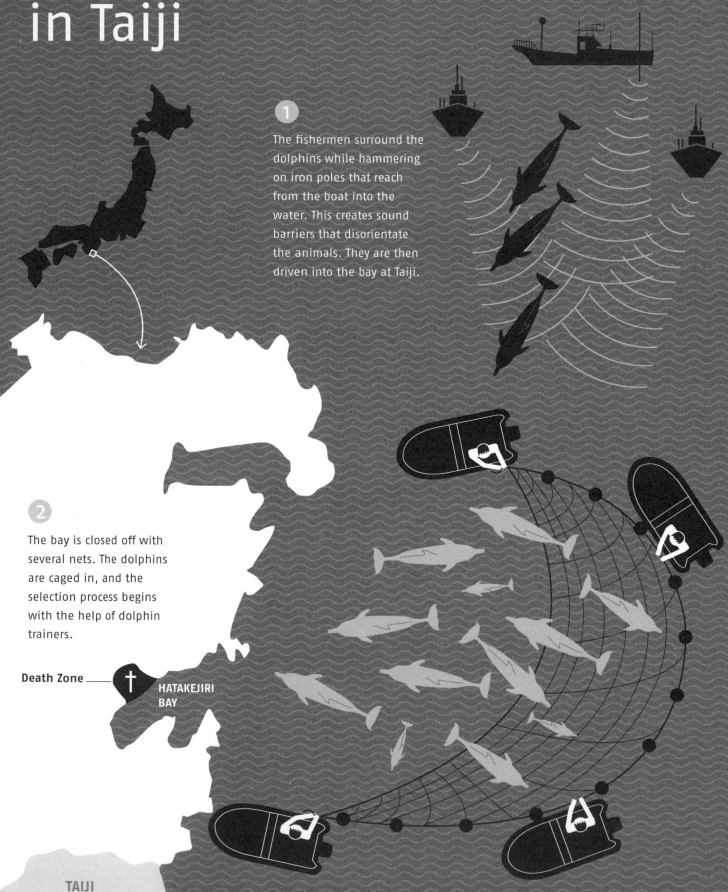

1

The fishermen surround the dolphins while hammering on iron poles that reach from the boat into the water. This creates sound barriers that disorientate the animals. They are then driven into the bay at Taiji.

2

The bay is closed off with several nets. The dolphins are caged in, and the selection process begins with the help of dolphin trainers.

Death Zone

HATAKEJIRI BAY

TAIJI

$200 000

③ Individual dolphins who look cute and have no scars are chosen to be trained. Dolphinariums around the world pay from 35 000 to 250 000 US dollars for such a dolphin.

Taiji is the biggest supplier of dolphins for aquariums and dolphin swimming programmes worldwide. From September 2015 to March 2016, 117 dolphins were captured alive there to be trained and sold.

④ All other dolphins are brutally stabbed to death with metal spears pierced right below the head. A dead dolphin is worth 600 US dollars. According to official quotas, up to 20 000 dolphins are killed in Japanese waters annually. Despite high levels of mercury pollution, dolphins are often sold as whale meat in Japanese supermarkets, or turned into fertiliser or animal feed.

⑤ Mercury is the most poisonous, non-radioactive substance for humans and mammals in the world. The methyl mercury concentration is very low in the ocean, but is absorbed by algae and thus enters the food chain. With every step up the food chain, the mercury concentration can increase up to tenfold. Dolphins are at the top of the marine food chain. In Taiji, methyl mercury rates in dolphins sold for food were found to be 5 000 times higher than what the United Nations (UN) deems safe for consumption.

Sources: ceta-base (2012), Sea Shepherd (2016)

Sea turtles in danger

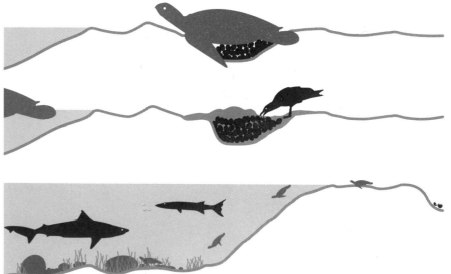

Sea turtles usually return to the beach of their birth to lay up to 1000 eggs. On average, only one of those 1000 eggs will live to reach maturity. The eggs remain buried in the sand, unprotected and easy pickings for coyotes, dogs, birds and poachers. The hawksbill turtle reaches maturity between the ages of 20 and 40.

Sources: Brewer et al. (2006), CWBR (2017), Haine et al. (2005), Lewison et al. (2014)

By-catch intensity: low ▪▪▪▪▪ high   trawl   gill net   long lines

80 million tons of catch are annually hauled to land from the sea, of which an estimated 30% is by-catch—including sea turtles—that gets thrown overboard, dead or injured.

Sea turtles are not only by-catch. Sometimes they are targeted for their meat or shells—often illegally. Many sea turtles die by getting entangled in plastic garbage or by confusing plastic bags with their main food, jellyfish.

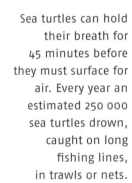

Sea turtles can hold their breath for 45 minutes before they must surface for air. Every year an estimated 250 000 sea turtles drown, caught on long fishing lines, in trawls or nets.

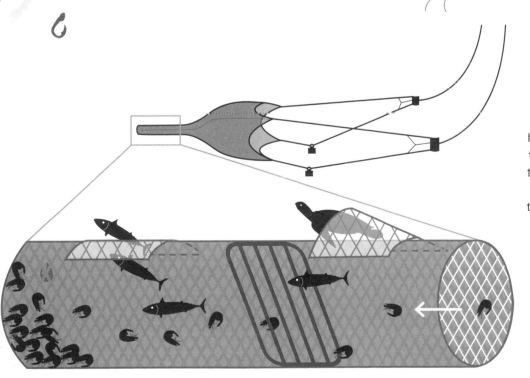

In Australia, by-catch casualties of sea turtles have reduced by 90% since the introduction of shrimp trawls that include exits for turtles and fish to escape through. Shrimp are caught at the back of the net and cannot escape because of the speed of the trawls being pulled through the water. The contraption also aids fishermen, since about 40% of the shrimp are otherwise squashed to death by the by-catch.

Aquaculture in numbers

Almost 50% of the 167 million tons of fish products worldwide now come from aquaculture industries.

Global fish production from aquaculture

8 million tons

1985

74 million tons

2014

Rest of the world
11%

Rest of Asia
27%

China
62%

89% of the world's aquaculture production is located in Asia, with 62% coming from China alone.

Sources: FAO (2016), Maribus (2013)

5

Antibiotics were found in farmed fish

- Oxytetracycline
- 4-Epioxytetracycline
- Sulfadimethoxine
- Ormetoprim
- Virginiamycin

Salmon

Tilapia

Trout

Shrimp

approx. **600** different species—including algae, sponges, molluscs, prawns, fishes and frogs—are farmed in aquaculture facilities around the globe.

2.3 kg of feed is needed per 1 kg (2.2lb) of edible carp.

(5 lb)

(Feed needed per 1 kg (2.2lb) of edible product)

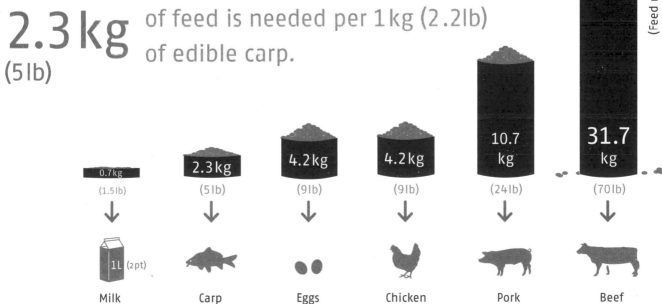

0.7kg	2.3kg	4.2kg	4.2kg	10.7 kg	31.7 kg
(1.5lb)	(5lb)	(9lb)	(9lb)	(24lb)	(70lb)
↓	↓	↓	↓	↓	↓
1L (2pt)					
Milk	Carp	Eggs	Chicken	Pork	Beef

Industrial aquaculture

Artificial reproduction

Eggs are artificially inseminated, then monitored in the laboratory and sorted. When the young fish are 30 days old they are transferred from spawning dishes into rearing tanks.

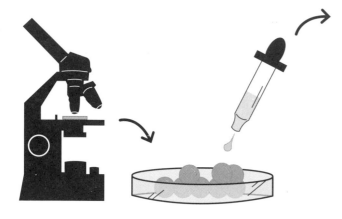

Rearing in tank farms

Tight quarters and loud pumps have the fish in a constant state of stress, resulting in their eating less, growing slower and being more susceptible to disease. Since disease spreads rapidly in these tanks, the fish are fed antibiotics as a preventative measure.

Traditional	Alternatives
Fish oil	Soy/Rapeseed oil
Fishmeal	Insect larvae meal

Water purification

Through several steps, coarse particles are filtered out of the water, which is then run through finer biological filters, enriched with oxygen and sterilised with UV lights, before it is pumped back into the fish tanks. Consequently, the water in the tanks is constantly in motion.

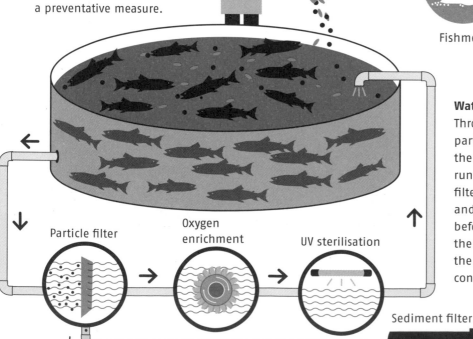

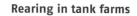

Particle filter   Oxygen enrichment   UV sterilisation

Sediment filter

Sources: Maribus (2013), FAO (2014)

Aquaculture in the ocean

The cages are covered
with nets to protect
the fish from seabirds.
The fish are fed through
machines in the middle
of the cage.

Other types

Filter-feeding bivalves
and seaweed are grown
on lines hanging in
the water. The organisms
take nutrition from the
surrounding ocean water,
or filter plankton organisms
from the water. Thus there
is no need for additional
fertiliser or feed.

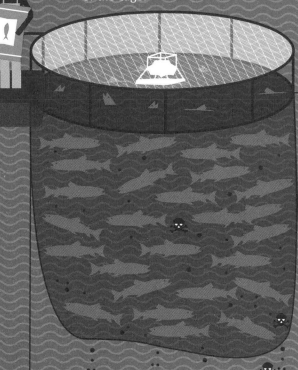

Choice of location

The cages are installed
in safe bays, where
they can be swiftly
accessed by boat and
are not subject to strong
currents or winds. Uneaten
foods and fish excrement
collect below the cages
and over-fertilise the bay.
Antibiotic residue also gets
into the water and can
damage the ecosystem and
its inhabitants.

Aquaculture is the captive breeding of aquatic
organisms, including fish, bivalves, crabs
and algae.

Aquaculture has its pros and cons. It can fulfil
the world's need for protein, while sometimes
also being environmentally and animal-friendly,
as in the cases of tilapia and carp. But there is
also considerable criticism: aquaculture is often
compared to poultry factory farming, due to
the close quarters and resulting stress. Aquatic
creatures cannot move according to their nature
and are bred and survive only with the help of
antibiotics. The waste waters from these cultures
over-fertilise rivers and bays, even though they
are slight in comparison to pesticide-rich, agricultural waste waters.

A combination of fish and shell-based marine
aquaculture can balance out certain drawbacks:
bivalves filter out algae that become invasive
through the influx of nutrients, reducing the
negative side effects of over-fertilisation. However, they also store pollutants from plankton
and antibiotics in their tissue.

Fish farming of the future

The aquaponic system

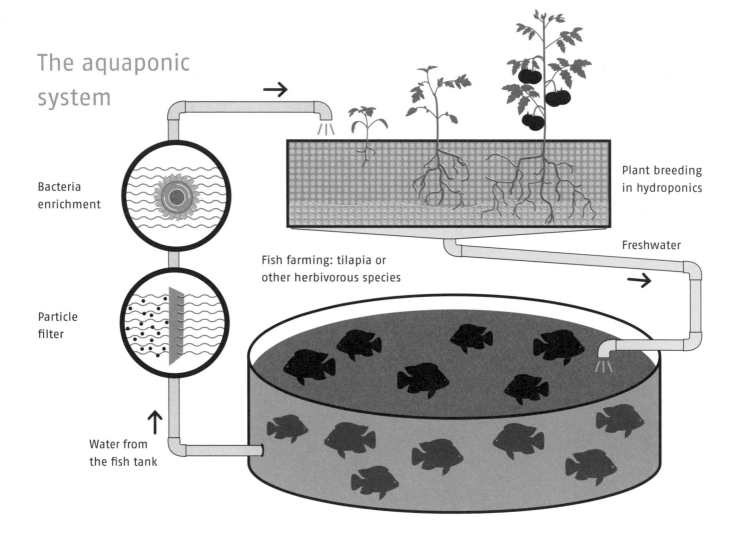

Bacteria enrichment

Particle filter

Water from the fish tank

Fish farming: tilapia or other herbivorous species

Plant breeding in hydroponics

Freshwater

It is a near perfect circuit: "soiled" fish water is pumped almost directly from tanks to farms growing tomatoes or other plants. Coarser particles are removed and bacteria are added to the mix, which aid the plants in absorbing nutrients. This naturally-generated fertiliser feeds the plants, allowing them to grow faster and with a higher yield, while purifying the water as a positive side effect, which is then given back to the fishes. The plants add enough nutrients to the water, so that the food organisms for the fish can develop sufficiently, drastically reducing and sometimes eliminating a farm's need to put in additional feed. The plants lower the rate of CO_2 consumption as well, because the filtration technology uses considerably less electricity. Fewer fish per tank and higher standards of hygiene relieve stress and lower the risk of disease, making the use of antibiotics in a preventative manner unnecessary.

In this way fish farming can be sustainable and environmentally friendly. Aquaponics are currently being researched, but remain quite rare on an industrial scale around the world.

Source: DFO (2013), Maribus (2013)

Integrated multi-tropic aquaculture (IMTA)

The caged salmon is the only species in the system which requires additional feed. Their excretions and left-overs provide nutrients for a whole slew of other organisms.

Fish excrement and food leftovers float over to bivalves and seaweed grown next to the fish enclosure, where nutrients are absorbed in turn, with food particles filtered out from the "waste".

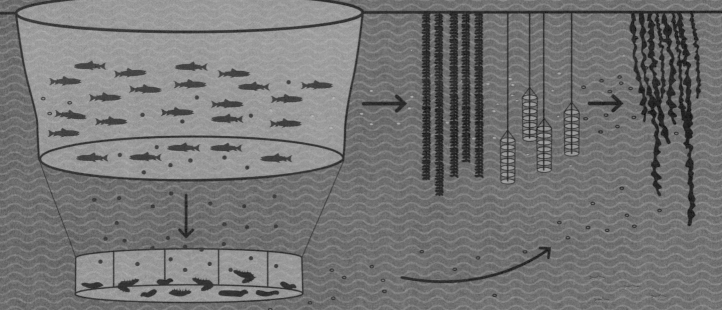

Some of the excess fish food and excrement sink down and are eaten by sea cucumbers held in a cage below the fish.

IMTA alleviates negative side effects associated with aquaculture, such as over-fertilisation, keeping the local ecosystem around farms in balance. This new type of aquaculture is well on its way to shaping the future of the industry, because it is also more economical: equal amounts of feed and space give higher yields and a wider variety of products to offer on the market. The system follows the principles of a permaculture endeavour, the opposite of monoculture, meaning that instead of just farming a single species, an entire community is raised. Researchers are now trying to identify what additional organisms can complete an IMTA system.

The last of the nutrients sink to the ocean floor, where they can increase algae growth. This algae coverage is then grazed on by sea urchins, for example.

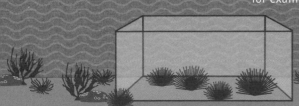

Illegal fishing

By definition, illegal fishing takes place when fishing vessels go out and fish in the territorial waters of other nations without authorization, when fishing legislation, fishing seasons or protected areas are ignored, or when catch and landing are not registered and reported.

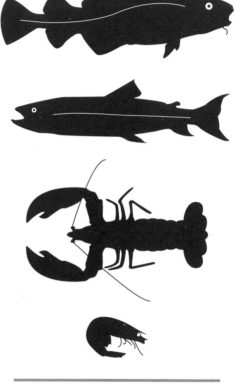

Illegal catch is estimated at 20 to 32 million tons globally a year

Legal catch ranges from 80 to 90 million tons globally a year

Expensive overfished varieties are often the object of illegal fishing efforts. In the northern hemisphere these are mostly codfish, salmon and lobster, while in the southern hemisphere ground-dwelling species such as crayfish and shrimp are targeted. In this way an estimated 10 to 23 billion US dollars are made circumventing all government taxation and fishing regulations.

$10–23 billion a year

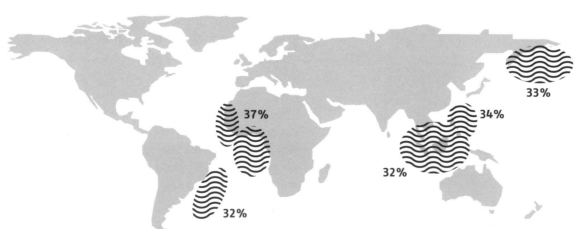

37%

32%

32%

34%

33%

Illegal fishing hot spots: Scientists estimate that from 2000 to 2003 approximately 32 to 37% of all catch in these regions was fished illegally.

Global percentage
of flag of convenience countries
participating in shipping:
vessels with a gross tonnage
of 1000 and upward

2012
72%

2009
69%

1999
61%

1989
42%

Sailing under
a "flag of conveni-
ence" is a booming
trend. The ship owner
could come from
Finland, for exam-
ple, but register his
boat in Panama. In
this way he can avoid
EU wage guidelines,
laws, taxes and regu-
lated fishing quotas.

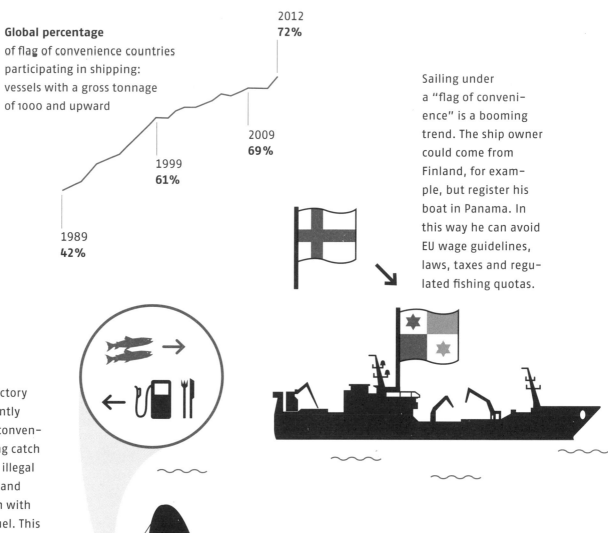

Over 700 big factory
ships are currently
flying flags of conven-
ience, collecting catch
from legal and illegal
fishing vessels and
providing them with
supplies and fuel. This
procedure is known
as "transshipping".
With it, smaller fish-
ing vessels are able to
operate continuously,
without having to call
on their port of registry
or declare their catch.
This saves money, fuel
and time.

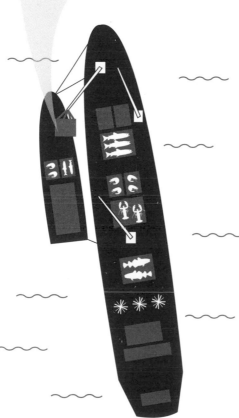

Illegal, unregistered and unregulated fishing
puts more pressure on already fragile fish
populations. In addition, smaller traditional
fishermen, especially in poorer countries, are
coming home empty-handed at an ever increasing rate, because their territorial waters are
illegally fished by industrial scale operations.
Developing nations who cannot afford to
have or maintain their own coastal guard are
especially affected. Illegal catch is often landed
in harbours with no surveillance authorities or
located in countries that are particularly susceptible to corruption. Only a fraction, if any, of
this catch is ever declared. Illegally-caught fish is
most commonly brought in by vessels sailing
under flags of convenience and are not included
in any statistics. This makes it extremely hard to
estimate populations and the current degree of
risk for many species of fish. While these problems
are largely confined to third-world and fast-
developing nations, ultimately most of the
illegally caught fish ends up being exported to
industrial nations.

Sources: Agnew et al. (2009), Maribus (2013), UNCTAD (2013)

"The experiences
of the USA and Norway,
for example,
suggest that science-based
governance of fisheries can
rebuild previously depleted stocks.
Also, catch quota can be
adjusted so that the biomass
of exploited stocks is kept at levels
that reduce the risk
of collapse, and fisheries can be
profitable even when
not subsidised."

Prof Daniel Pauly,
University of British Columbia
Vancouver, Canada

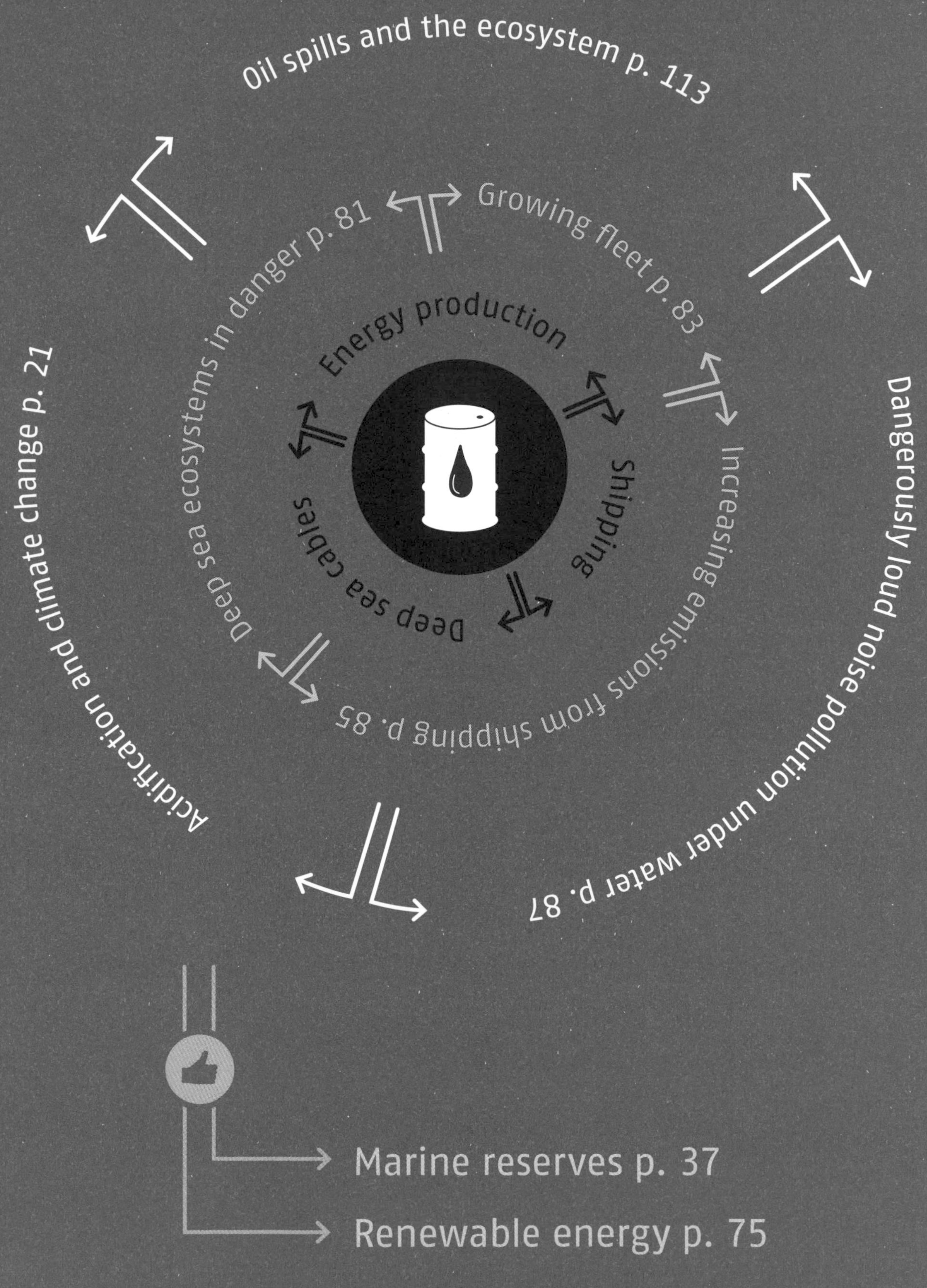
Energy production
Shipping
Deep sea cables
Growing fleet p. 83
Increasing emissions from shipping p. 85
Deep sea ecosystems in danger p. 81
Oil spills and the ecosystem p. 113
Dangerously loud noise pollution under water p. 87
Acidification and climate change p. 21
Marine reserves p. 37
Renewable energy p. 75

Ocean-based industries

Energy from the ocean

The off-shore wind farming capacity keeps growing

Worldwide, in megawatts per year

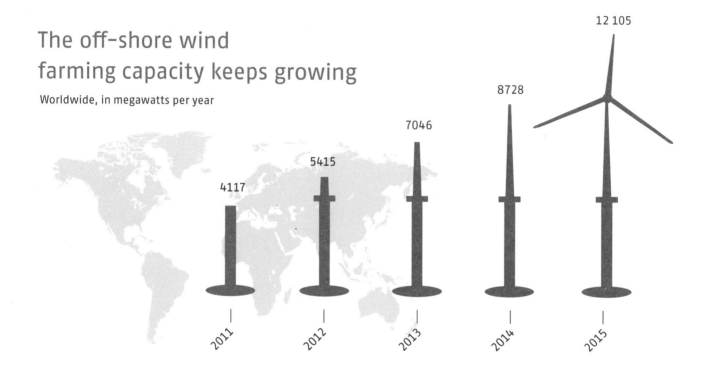

4117 — 2011
5415 — 2012
7046 — 2013
8728 — 2014
12 105 — 2015

"30 percent of oil and natural gases already come from deposits below the ocean floor." Prof Hartmut Grassl, Max Planck Institute, Hamburg

Prognosis

for offshore oil and gas production in the Atlantic

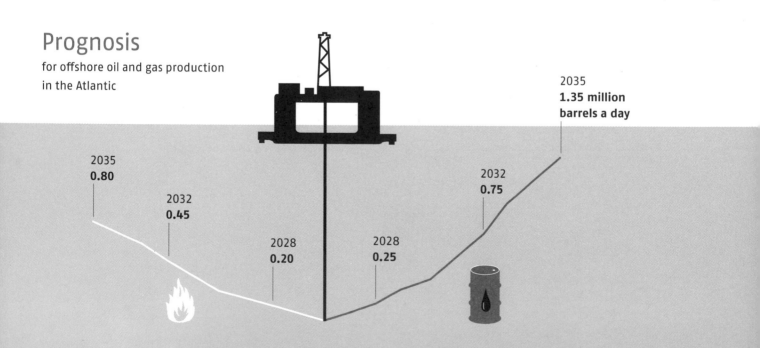

2035
0.80

2032
0.45

2028
0.20

2028
0.25

2032
0.75

2035
1.35 million barrels a day

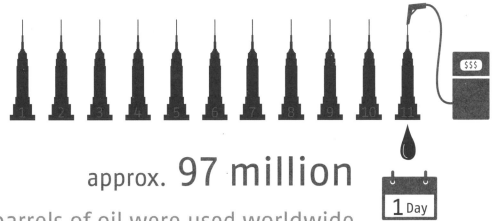

approx. 97 million

barrels of oil were used worldwide
every day in 2016. With these amounts,
you could fill the Empire State Building
eleven times over every day.

Primary energy sources

worldwide, 2014

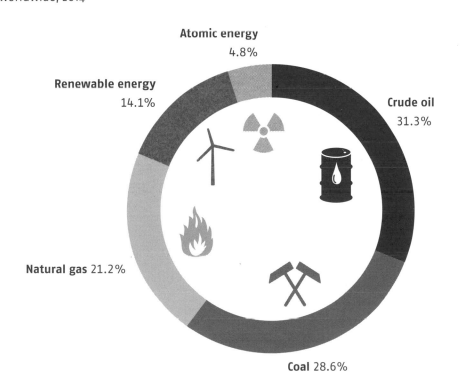

Atomic energy
4.8%

Renewable energy
14.1%

Crude oil
31.3%

Natural gas 21.2%

Coal 28.6%

The most
important source
of energy
worldwide is oil.
In the future it
will increasingly
come from
offshore oil rigs.

Sources: CIA (2015), EIA (2017), GWEC (2016), OECD/IEA (2015), Quest Offshore (2013)

Increase in offshore wind energy

The number of offshore wind parks is growing worldwide. In 2015 their global capacity amounted to approximately 12 100 megawatts. With over 90% of the globe's wind farms located in Northern Europe, the region can certainly be considered a leader and pioneer in this innovative technology.

Though the noise level and construction involved can increase stress on local ecosystems for a period, the positive effects clearly outweigh the negative: their high level of efficiency indirectly leads to a decrease in the need for fossil fuel-generating facilities, decreasing global CO_2 emissions, slowing down some of the main contributors to climate change, and finally improving air quality and thus human health in general.

Fishing is prohibited around these wind farms, and artificial reefs form on their foundations, increasing biodiversity.

Theoretically, up to **10** nuclear power plants can already be replaced by the global installation of offshore wind parks with their current capacity of 12 100 megawatts.

When offshore wind power plants are built there is a temporary increase in noise levels under water, sediment billows up in clouds and the sea bed is compressed as the foundations are rammed into the ground.

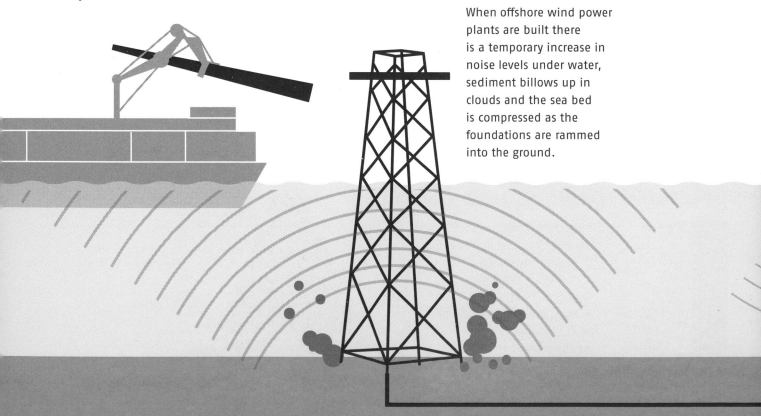

Sources: EWEA (2016), Gill (2005), James (2013), Langhamer (2012), Wahlberg (2005), Zeiler (2005)

The noise created by the rotor blades continues as a vibration all the way down into the foundations. Today there are already rotor blades that operate with nearly no sound whatsoever.

Because fishing is prohibited around offshore wind farms, it is the perfect environment for strongly overfished populations to recover.

In addition, over time "artificial" reefs start forming around their foundations. This promotes biodiversity, but it can also open the door to invasive species.

Depending on wind speeds, some amount of rumbling can be heard at different levels under water.
Its effect on marine life has yet to be subject to any significant research.

The cables that transport the electricity generated by the windmills to land are buried three metres deep. They heat up and thus also heat up the ground around them, potentially disrupting the local ecosystem and species living on the seabed.

Waves and tides – energy of the future?

The "SeaGen F" tidal stream generator floating on the surface, and the "Open Centre" turbine installed under water, were both tested in Fundy Bay, Canada.

The floating "Pelamis" wave energy converter was tested in Peniche, Portugal and off Scotland's Orkney Islands.

Tidal stream generators are highly effective if located where tidal currents are especially strong. They can be installed on the seabed or floating on the water's surface. The turbines transform the currents' horizontal movement into kinetic energy.

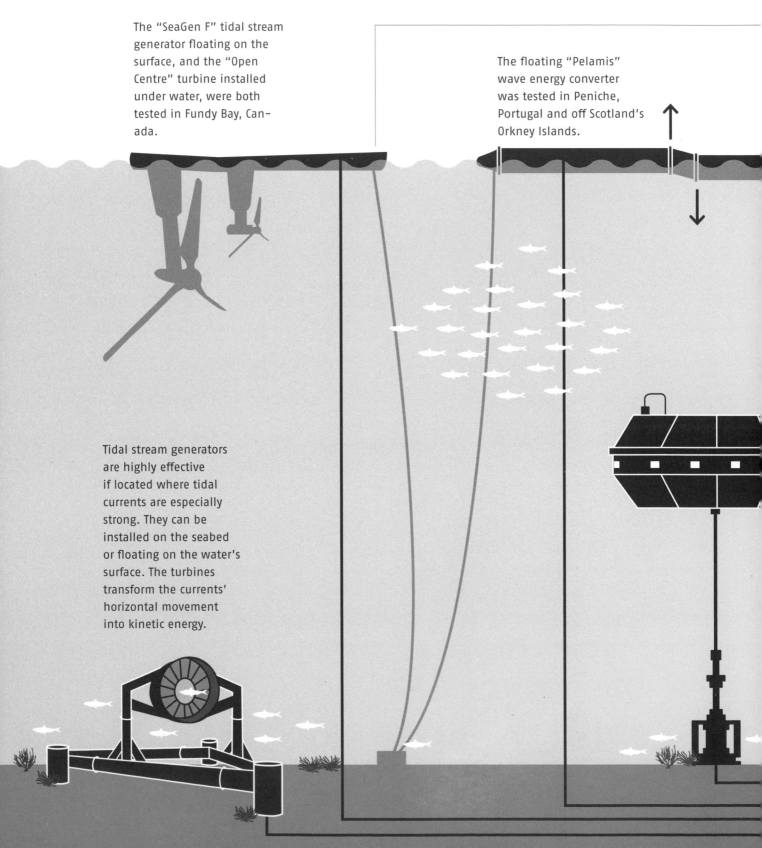

Pilot projects around the world

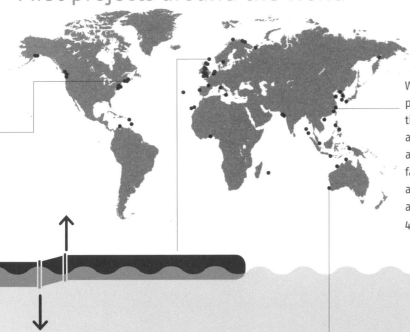

With one power plant based on tidal range as well as seven other tidal and wave energy facilities, China is able to generate a capacity of over 4100 megawatts.

On land, hydrodynamic energy is transformed through pumps, turbines and generators, first into mechanical, then hydraulic and finally electrical energy.

Strong winds on the high seas produce waves that ride all the way to the coast where they can be harvested to generate wave energy. The structures can be either under water or floating on the surface. So far there are 25 different types of plants being tested around the world. The stronger the wind, the greater the energy of the waves. Thus ideal locations are the western coasts of Europe, South America and Australia.

The wave energy generator "CETO" was tested both in Perth, Australia, as well as off the French island of La Réunion.

"Only few bays and canals have tidal currents strong enough to be harvested for commercial use."
Prof Hartmut Grassl, Max Planck Institute, Hamburg

Sources: WEC (2013), OES (2014)

Raw material reserves of the deep sea

Manganese nodules are formed on the seabed at 4000–6500m (13 000–21 000ft) and take millions of years to grow just a few millimetres. These nodules of 5–10 cm (2–4in) in size contain valuable industrial metals such as manganese, iron, nickel, copper, lithium and cobalt. Lithium, for example, is used in cellular and laptop batteries.

Volcanogenic massive sulphides are formed where tectonic plates drift apart at 500–5000m (1650–16 500ft) depth. They contain copper, zinc and gold, among other things. So far only a few places are known where mining these reserves is commercially viable, such as the Manus Basin in the South Western Pacific.

Occurring as of 400m (1300ft) below the surface — Oil — Natural gas — Massive sulphides — Manganese nodules — Cobalt crusts

Cobalt crusts grow even slower than manganese nodules, at any depth, on stone surfaces free of sediment such as underwater rock cliffs or mountains. They are mostly made of manganese and iron and contain small amounts of commercially interesting elements such as nickel, cobalt, copper, titanium, and rare earths. The last are utilised in the production of mobile phones, flat screens, hybrid vehicles and wind turbines.

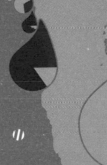

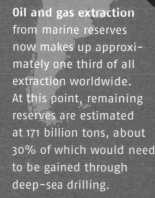

Oil and gas extraction from marine reserves now makes up approximately one third of all extraction worldwide. At this point, remaining reserves are estimated at 171 billion tons, about 30% of which would need to be gained through deep-sea drilling.

Sources: GEOMAR (2016), Maribus (2014), Rona (2003), UBA (2013), UNEP (2013)

Deep-sea mining

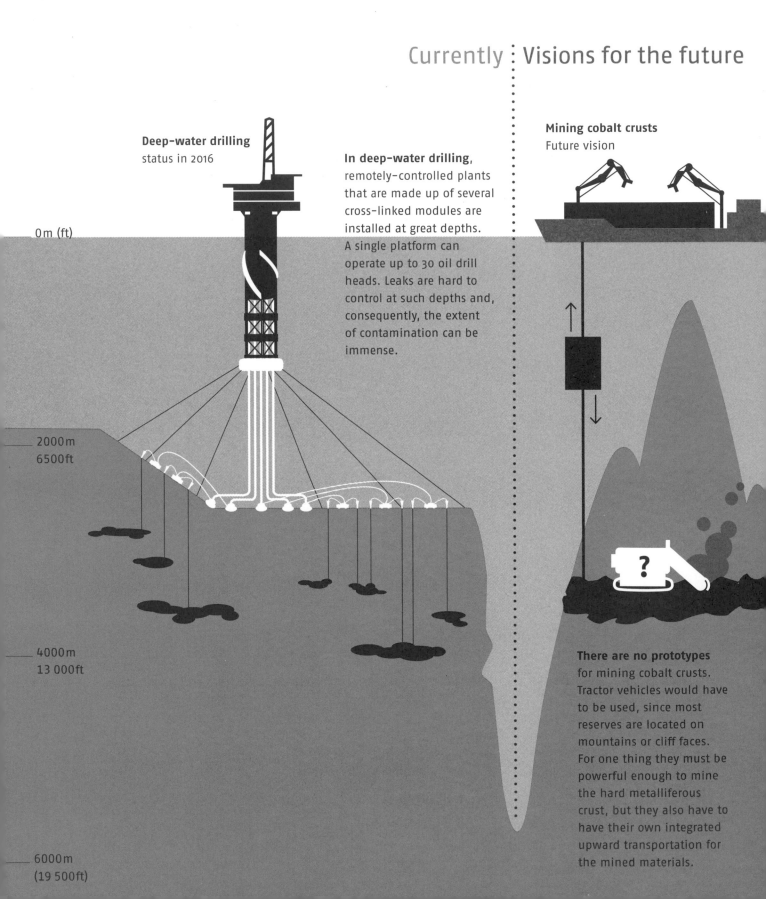

Currently : Visions for the future

Deep-water drilling
status in 2016

Mining cobalt crusts
Future vision

In deep-water drilling, remotely-controlled plants that are made up of several cross-linked modules are installed at great depths. A single platform can operate up to 30 oil drill heads. Leaks are hard to control at such depths and, consequently, the extent of contamination can be immense.

There are no prototypes for mining cobalt crusts. Tractor vehicles would have to be used, since most reserves are located on mountains or cliff faces. For one thing they must be powerful enough to mine the hard metalliferous crust, but they also have to have their own integrated upward transportation for the mined materials.

0m (ft)

2000m
6500ft

4000m
13 000ft

6000m
(19 500ft)

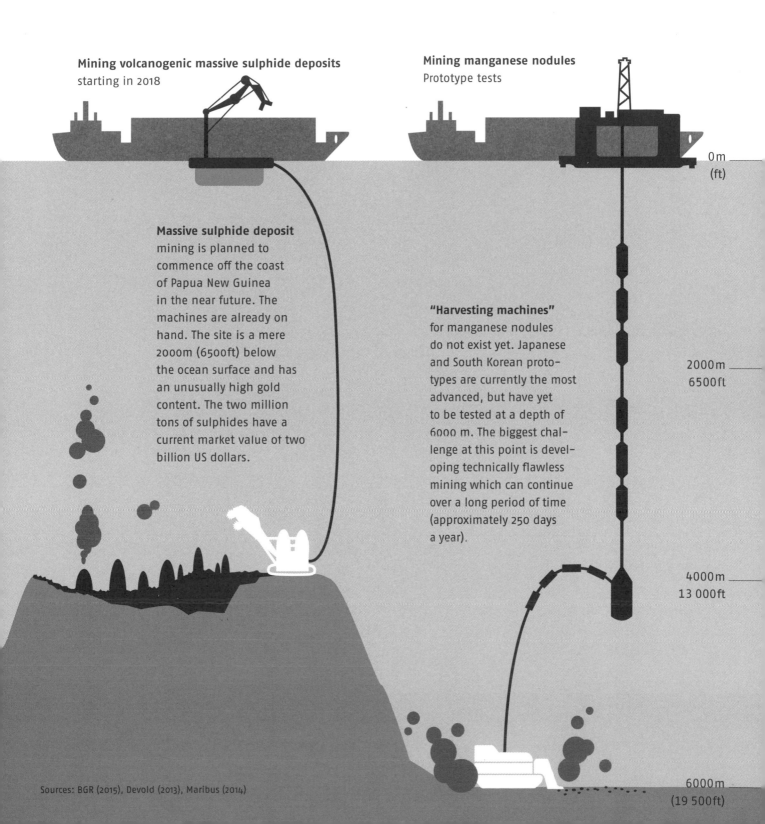

Mining volcanogenic massive sulphide deposits
starting in 2018

Mining manganese nodules
Prototype tests

0 m
(ft)

Massive sulphide deposit
mining is planned to
commence off the coast
of Papua New Guinea
in the near future. The
machines are already on
hand. The site is a mere
2000m (6500ft) below
the ocean surface and has
an unusually high gold
content. The two million
tons of sulphides have a
current market value of two
billion US dollars.

"Harvesting machines"
for manganese nodules
do not exist yet. Japanese
and South Korean proto-
types are currently the most
advanced, but have yet
to be tested at a depth of
6000 m. The biggest chal-
lenge at this point is developing technically flawless
mining which can continue
over a long period of time
(approximately 250 days
a year).

2000m
6500ft

4000m
13 000ft

6000m
(19 500ft)

Sources: BGR (2015), Devold (2013), Maribus (2014)

Oceanic transport routes

 **91 GT** global commercial fleet 1955

1 800 000 000 dwt global commercial fleet 2015

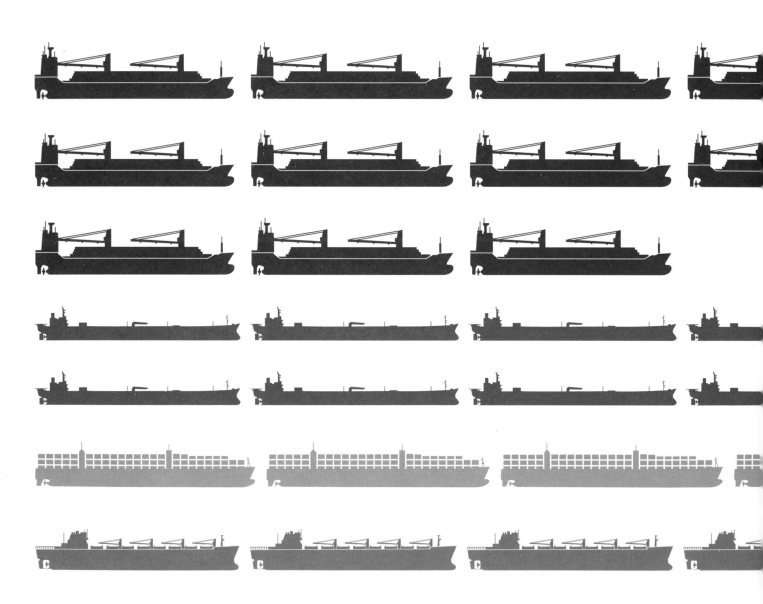

5 950 000 dwt ferries and passenger vessels

GT = Gross Tonnage
dwt = deadweight tonnage

80% of all global trade is procured by about 48 500 cargo
ships. They are the true engine of globalisation.
The increasing sizes of the ships lower transport costs
per container, while emissions rise as a whole.
Most cargo and cruise ships use heavy oils and have
no particulate filters. Sulphur, heavy metals and
particulate matter emitted contribute to health issues,
particularly in coastal areas.

1955

2015

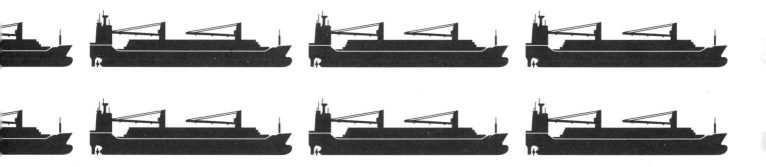

779 000 000 dwt general cargo ships

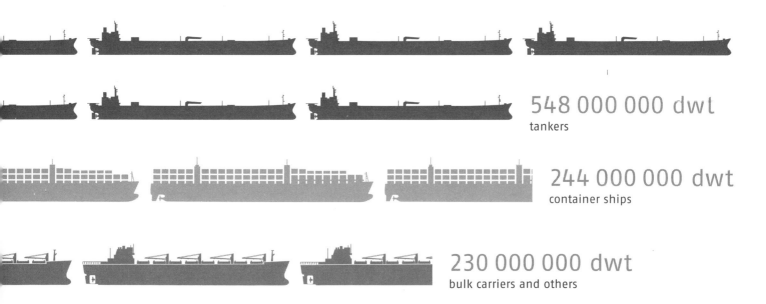

548 000 000 dwt
tankers

244 000 000 dwt
container ships

230 000 000 dwt
bulk carriers and others

Sources: KEG (1970), NABU (2014), UNCTAD (2016)

Harmful ship emissions

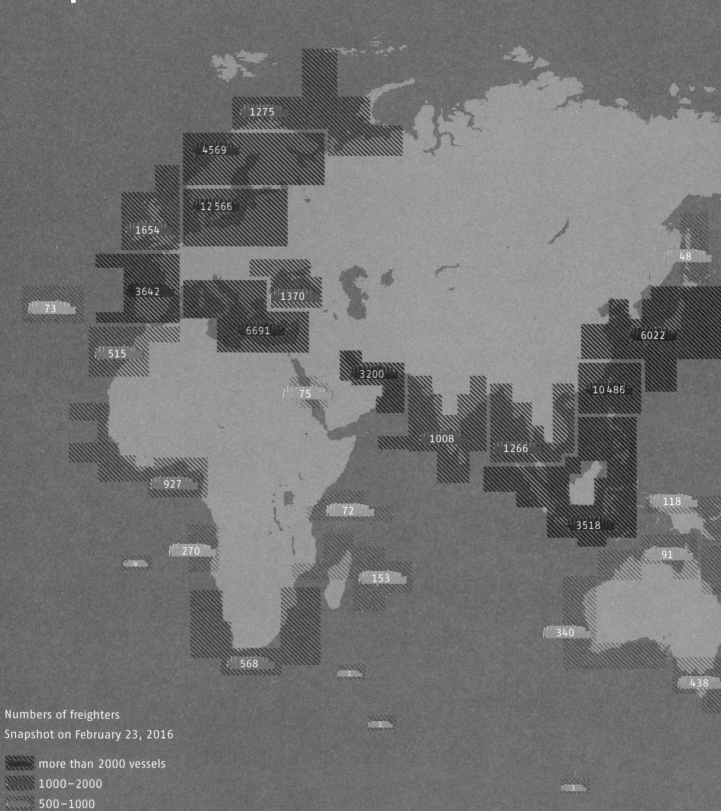

1275
4569
12 566
1654
48
3642
73
1370
6691
6022
515
10 486
3200
75
1008
1266
927
118
72
3518
270
91
4
153
340
568
1
438
1

Numbers of freighters
Snapshot on February 23, 2016

more than 2000 vessels
1000–2000
500–1000
1–500

Sources: Marine Traffic (2016), Corbett et al. (2007)

Global shipping density shows that most traffic hovers around the area within 400 km (250 mi) of the coast. 80% of all ship emissions are expelled in these zones.

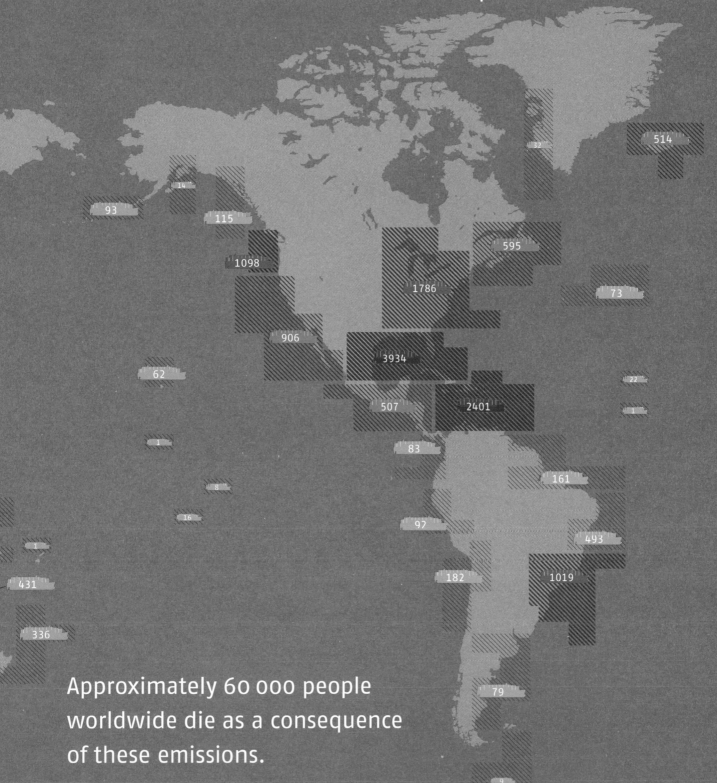

Approximately 60 000 people worldwide die as a consequence of these emissions.

A cruel cacophony

Increases in shipping traffic and seismic surveys have seen the level of noise in our oceans double every decade since 1950.

2010

For several years now, shipping activity in the St. Lawrence River in eastern Canada has increased, while the beluga whale population has dropped in parallel to this trend. To counteract this, a part of the river has been qualified as a Marine Conservation Area.

2000

Killer whales are so stressed by traffic around Vancouver Island that they increase their swimming speed whenever more than one ship is close by. This leads them to expend valuable energy needed to hunt for food.

1990

1980

1970

1960

1950

kph/mph

Sources: Jasny et al. (2005), Nowacek et al. (2001), Schorr et al. (2014), Veirs et al. (2016)

Dolphins change the duration of their dives and their habitats when they get too stressed by the noises of shipping traffic. In addition, their echolocation abilities are impaired by sonar interference.

Whales can get beached by disruptions to their navigation and hearing organs. Seismic exploration with air guns and submarines can render whales deaf. Thus impaired they are no longer able to find mates or food and may end up swimming about aimlessly.

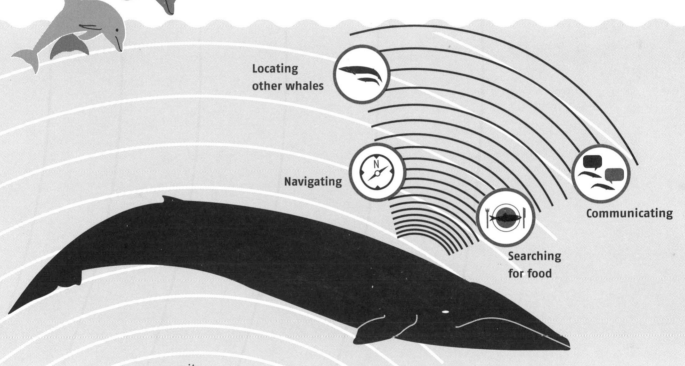

Locating other whales

Navigating

Communicating

Searching for food

Submarines with LFAS sonar emit sound waves of **100 to 500 Hertz** and a sound intensity of up to **230 decibels.** That is louder than a rocket engine at 180 decibels.

Low frequency active sonar (LFAS) is built into US Navy submarines. It is used to track near-silent nuclear submarines by projecting extremely loud low frequency sound waves into the open ocean.

"There is no question that sonar injures and kills whales and dolphins." Joel Reynolds, Natural Resources Defence Council (NRDC)

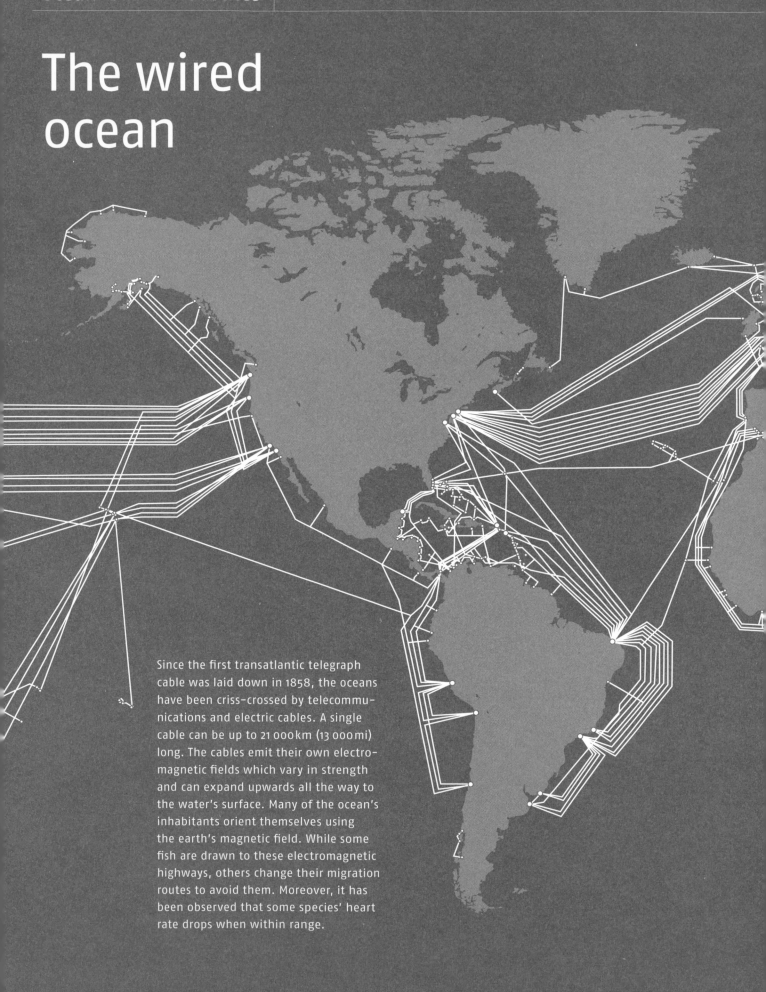

The wired ocean

Since the first transatlantic telegraph cable was laid down in 1858, the oceans have been criss-crossed by telecommunications and electric cables. A single cable can be up to 21 000 km (13 000 mi) long. The cables emit their own electromagnetic fields which vary in strength and can expand upwards all the way to the water's surface. Many of the ocean's inhabitants orient themselves using the earth's magnetic field. While some fish are drawn to these electromagnetic highways, others change their migration routes to avoid them. Moreover, it has been observed that some species' heart rate drops when within range.

—• Deep sea cables

99% of all global telephone and internet traffic currently passes through a network of approximately 420 ocean cables with a gross length of 1.1 million kilometres (.7 m mi).

Sources: Andrulewicz (2003), TG (2016), Starosielski (2015)

"The possibility of using the ocean
to harvest energy from renewable sources
such as wind, waves and tides is being
expanded on a global scale. Drilling
for oil and natural gas is happening in
ever deeper waters, and marine mining
is being explored in the deep seas,
even though these measures are not yet
necessary. If the world population
keeps growing, the corresponding increase
in the need for natural resources
will make the intensified use of
the deep seas inevitable. Finding
the right balance between their protection
and utilisation is one of the greatest
challenges we face over the next
few years."

Dr Sven Petersen,
co-editor of 'Encyclopedia of Marine Geosciences'

Causes → direct consequences → indirect consequences → approach to solutions

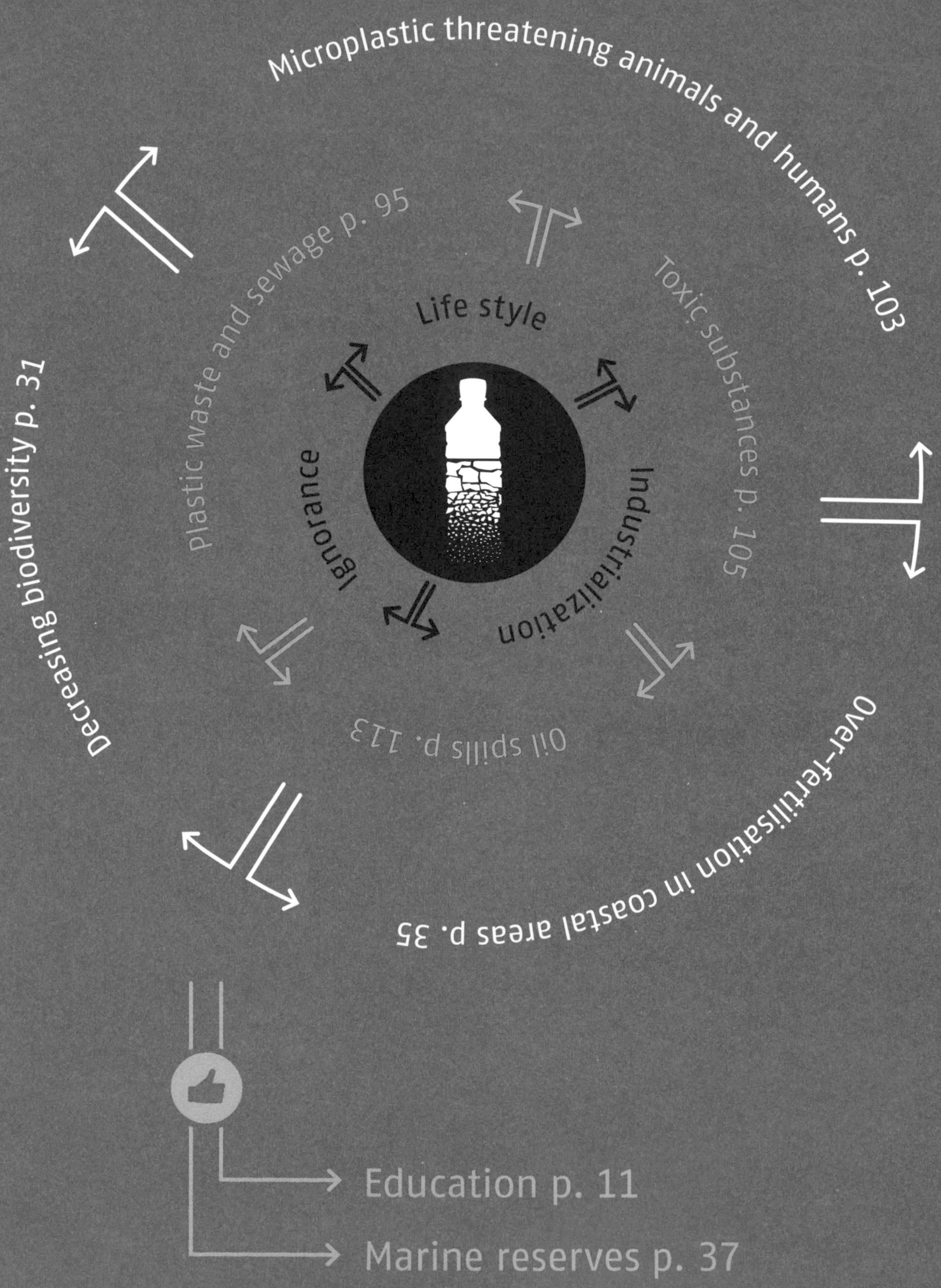
Microplastic threatening animals and humans p. 103
Decreasing biodiversity p. 31
Over-fertilisation in coastal areas p. 35
plastic waste and sewage p. 95
Toxic substances p. 105
Oil spills p. 113
Life style
Industrialization
Ignorance
Education p. 11
Marine reserves p. 37

Pollution

How does the ocean become polluted?

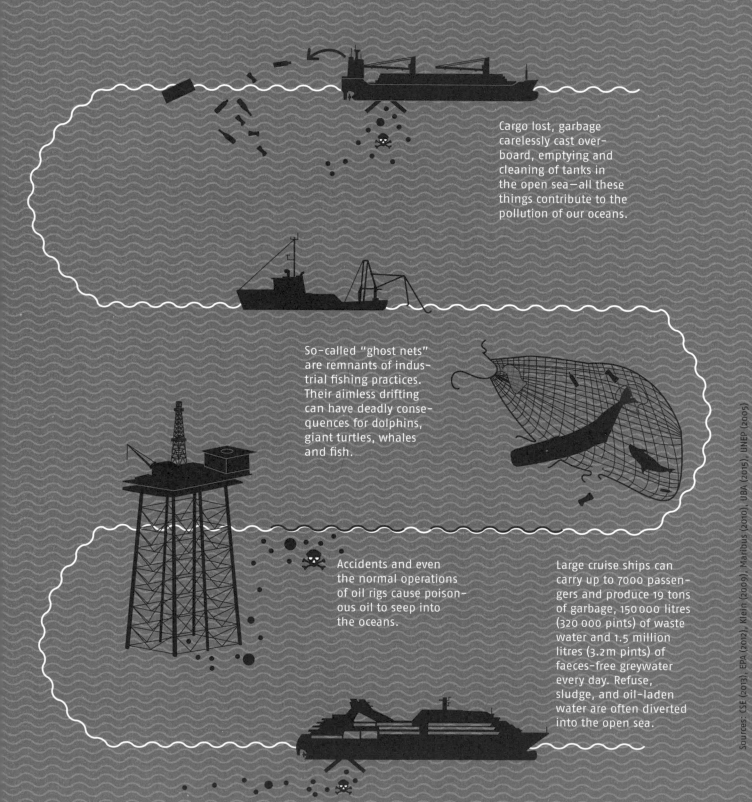

Cargo lost, garbage carelessly cast overboard, emptying and cleaning of tanks in the open sea—all these things contribute to the pollution of our oceans.

So-called "ghost nets" are remnants of industrial fishing practices. Their aimless drifting can have deadly consequences for dolphins, giant turtles, whales and fish.

Accidents and even the normal operations of oil rigs cause poisonous oil to seep into the oceans.

Large cruise ships can carry up to 7000 passengers and produce 19 tons of garbage, 150 000 litres (320 000 pints) of waste water and 1.5 million litres (3.2m pints) of faeces-free greywater every day. Refuse, sludge, and oil-laden water are often diverted into the open sea.

Sources: CSE (2013), EPA (2012), Klein (2009), Maribus (2010), UBA (2015), UNEP (2005)

Only approximately 20% of plastic ends up in the oceans directly...

Industrialised nations vs. developing nations

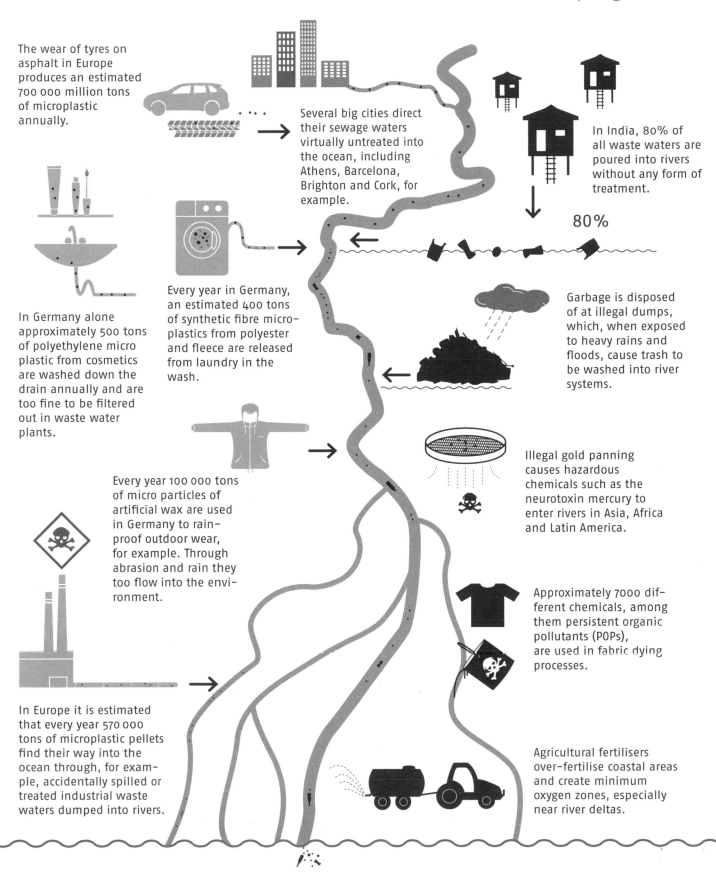

The wear of tyres on asphalt in Europe produces an estimated 700 000 million tons of microplastic annually.

Several big cities direct their sewage waters virtually untreated into the ocean, including Athens, Barcelona, Brighton and Cork, for example.

In India, 80% of all waste waters are poured into rivers without any form of treatment.

80%

In Germany alone approximately 500 tons of polyethylene micro plastic from cosmetics are washed down the drain annually and are too fine to be filtered out in waste water plants.

Every year in Germany, an estimated 400 tons of synthetic fibre micro-plastics from polyester and fleece are released from laundry in the wash.

Garbage is disposed of at illegal dumps, which, when exposed to heavy rains and floods, cause trash to be washed into river systems.

Every year 100 000 tons of micro particles of artificial wax are used in Germany to rain-proof outdoor wear, for example. Through abrasion and rain they too flow into the envi-ronment.

Illegal gold panning causes hazardous chemicals such as the neurotoxin mercury to enter rivers in Asia, Africa and Latin America.

Approximately 7000 dif-ferent chemicals, among them persistent organic pollutants (POPs), are used in fabric dying processes.

In Europe it is estimated that every year 570 000 tons of microplastic pellets find their way into the ocean through, for exam-ple, accidentally spilled or treated industrial waste waters dumped into rivers.

Agricultural fertilisers over-fertilise coastal areas and create minimum oxygen zones, especially near river deltas.

...while 80% reaches them indirectly through rivers.

Plastic garbage in the oceans

322 million tons

of plastic were produced
globally in 2015, and
the mountain of garbage
is growing every day.
A large part of all plastic
produced since 1950 has
found its way into our
dumps, landscapes, rivers
and oceans.

3-10%

of globally
collected plastic
is recycled.

Plastic
thrown away
after a single use: **33%**

Estimated time for degradation

| Paper bags 6 weeks | Plastic bags 1–20 years | Styrofoam packaging 50 years | Aluminium cans 200 years | Plastic bottles 200–450 years | Six pack rings 400 years | Fishing lines 600 years |

About **450 years** is the time it can take for a PET bottle to slowly break down into smaller fragments in the ocean, until they can no longer be seen by the naked eye. Plastic is a non–biodegradable material and, consequently, will never disappear entirely.

Over
100 000
marine mammals, sea birds and fishes die annually from consuming or getting caught in plastics.

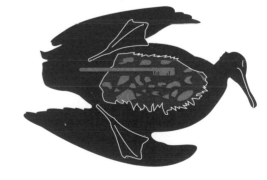

Sources: Schlining et al. (2013), PE (2016), Subba Reddy (2014), UNEP (2015), WEF (2016)

The five large garbage patches

Humans are responsible for them, while the ocean currents and winds form them: the five great plastic garbage patches floating in concentrated masses on the oceans, slowly breaking down into ever-smaller particles.

Plastic can now be found in all parts of the oceans, spreading into every nook and cranny, powered by the complex system of ocean currents. Plastic waste in the seas is estimated at 150 million tons, which is about a fifth of the weight of all fish. Scientists expect that by 2025 for every three tons of fish there will be one ton of plastic floating around. If we do not drastically reduce our plastic consumption, by 2050 the weight of plastic garbage in the ocean will be more than that of fish.

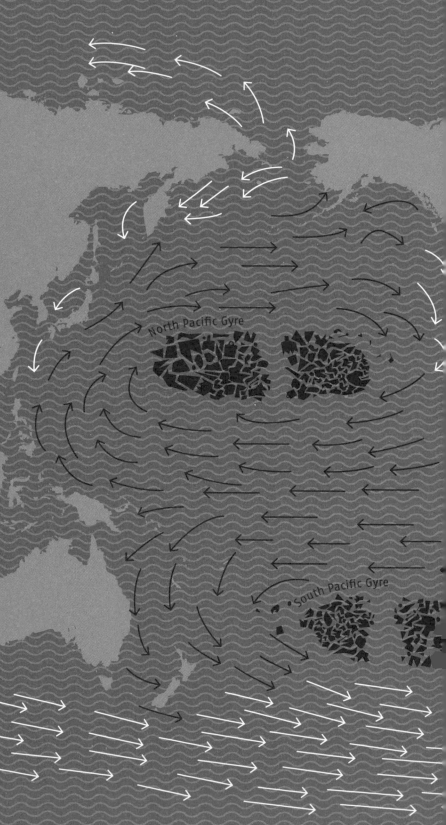

North Pacific Gyre

South Pacific Gyre

Indian Ocean Gyre

→ Warm ocean currents ⟶ Cold ocean currents 🖤 Gyres

Every minute an entire garbage truck
of plastic is dumped into the ocean somewhere
around the world—eight million tons per year!
If this trend continues, the amount of pollution
will quadruple by 2050.

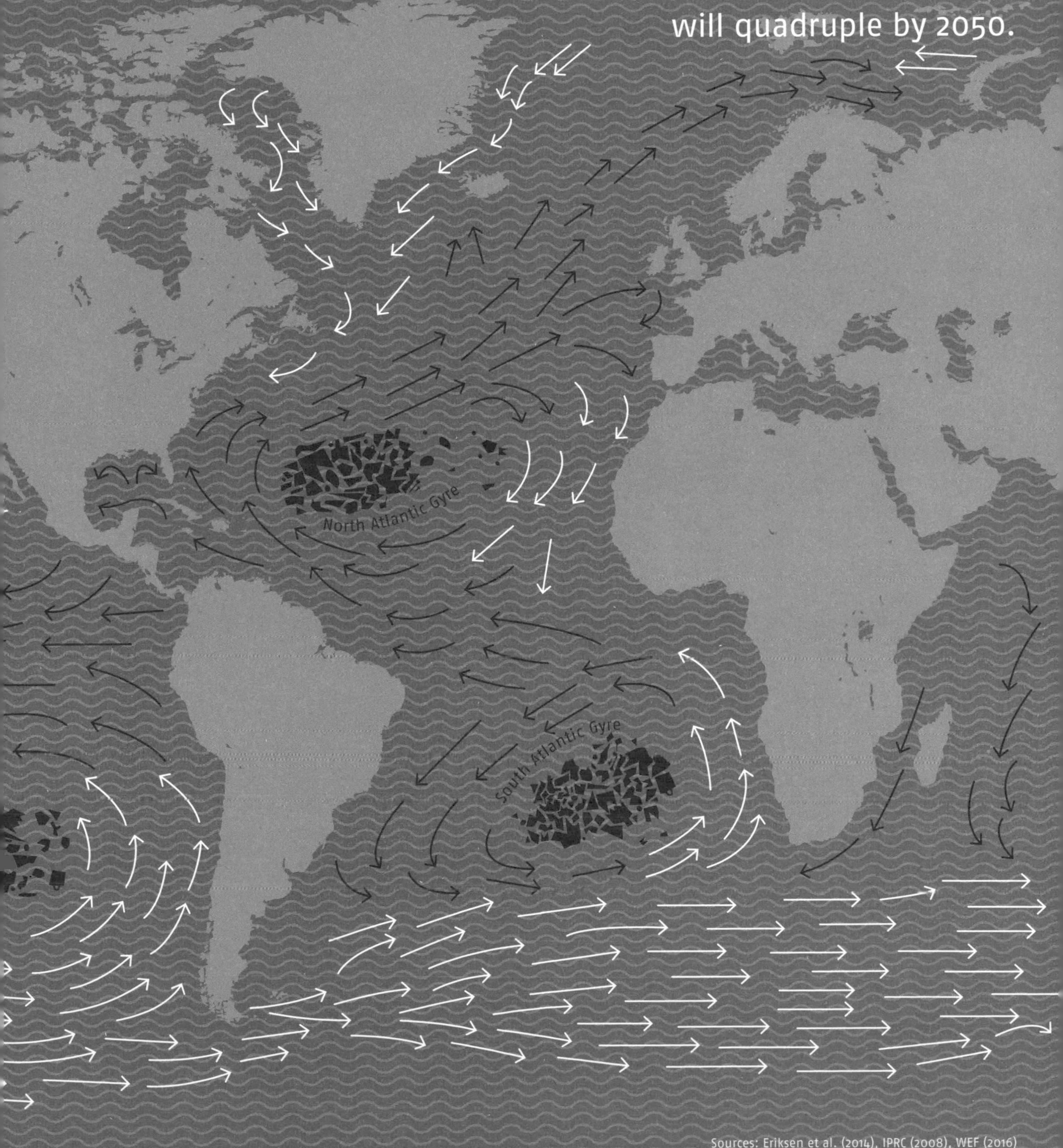

North Atlantic Gyre

South Atlantic Gyre

Sources: Eriksen et al. (2014), IPRC (2008), WEF (2016)

Cross section of a garbage patch

Trash floating visibly on the surface of the water can be compared to "the tip of the iceberg". The swirling mass of plastic can descend up to 30 metres into the depths of the ocean, a soup consisting of large to tiny particles. Sunlight, salinity and the water's constant movement make the plastics break down at varying speeds: it can be anything from 1 to 600 years until a plastic bag or fishing line has broken down into pieces the size of a grain of sand. A large part of it eventually sinks to the bottom of the ocean, settling on the sediment and eventually getting covered up by it. The highest density of synthetic material was found at the bottom of the ocean in Indonesia, with approximately 690 000 particles per square kilometre.

In the North Atlantic Gyre each kilo of zooplankton is matched by 6 kilos (13 lbs) of plastic

Sources: Eriksen (2014), GP (2007), ICC (2010), Moore (2001), Maribus (2010), UNEP (2005)

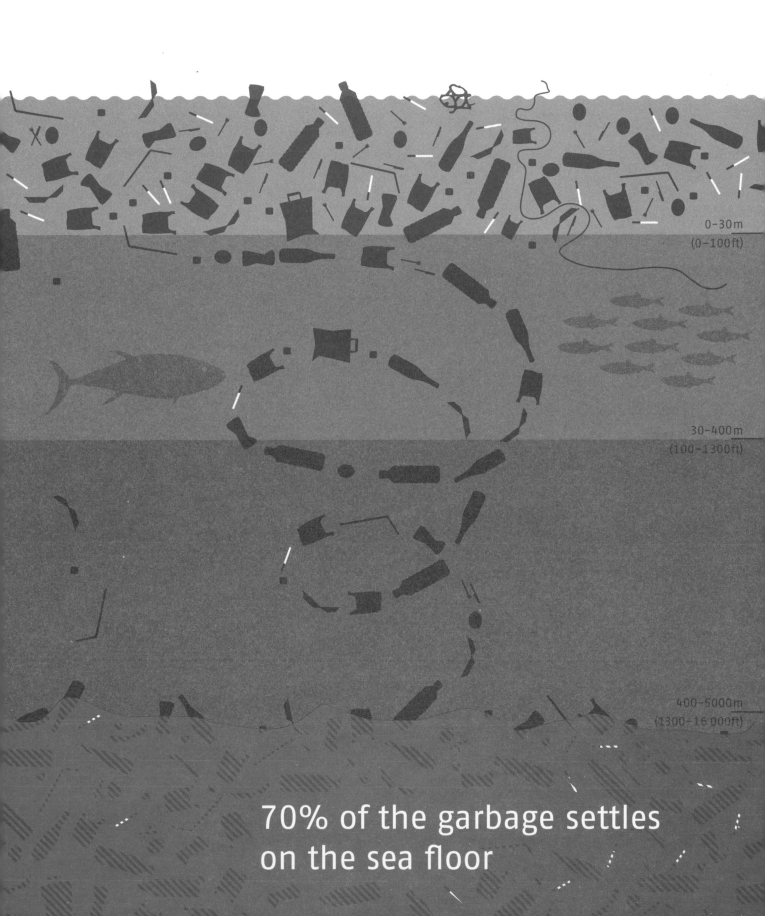

0–30m
(0–100ft)

30–400m
(100–1300ft)

400–5000m
(1300–16 000ft)

70% of the garbage settles
on the sea floor

Microplastics in the food chain

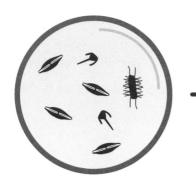

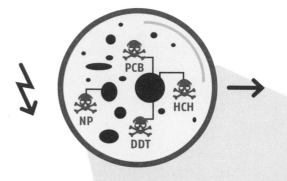

Phytoplankton
Single-cell plant organisms, mostly diatoms that live in the upper layers of the ocean and photosynthesize with the help of sunlight.

Zooplankton
Animal microorganisms such as krill that feed off phytoplankton. They are surrounded by microplastic particles that are similar in size.

Microplastics
Particles up to 5 millimetres in size that have fallen apart in the oceans over years, and that attract and bind with persistent organic pollutants (POPs).

Phytoplankton and zooplankton play a vital role in the ocean's ecosystems, because they form the basis of the food chain for nearly all life in the ocean. Since 1950, with the dawn of industrial fishing endeavours, the global zooplankton population has declined by around 40%. One reason for this is that zooplankton paste is increasingly used as a substitute for fishmeal to feed pigs, chickens and aquacultures in enormous farm plants. This has consequences for the sensitive ocean ecosystem. The bulk of oxygen produced by the ocean can be traced back to the phytoplankton's photosynthesis, whereby carbon dioxide is absorbed into plant biomass, expelling oxygen in the process.

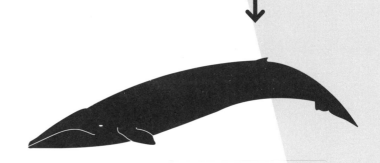

Blue whales
are the largest mammals on earth, growing up to lengths of 27-33m (90–110ft). With their baleen plates they filter krill from the water. Now, however, they inadvertently also consume toxic microplastics in the process.

Toxic substances in microplastic
Microplastic is washed up everywhere around the world and contains high concentrations of hazardous chemicals such as polychlorinated biphenyl (PCB). The map shows the highest concentrations of PCB in the world, measured in nanograms per gram of microplastic.

Sources: IPW (2015), Rios (2007), Van Cauwenberghe et al. (2014)

"A single plastic microbead becomes highly toxic while absorbing pollutants, and delivers them to marine life when ingested." Dr Marcus Eriksen, 5 Gyres Institute

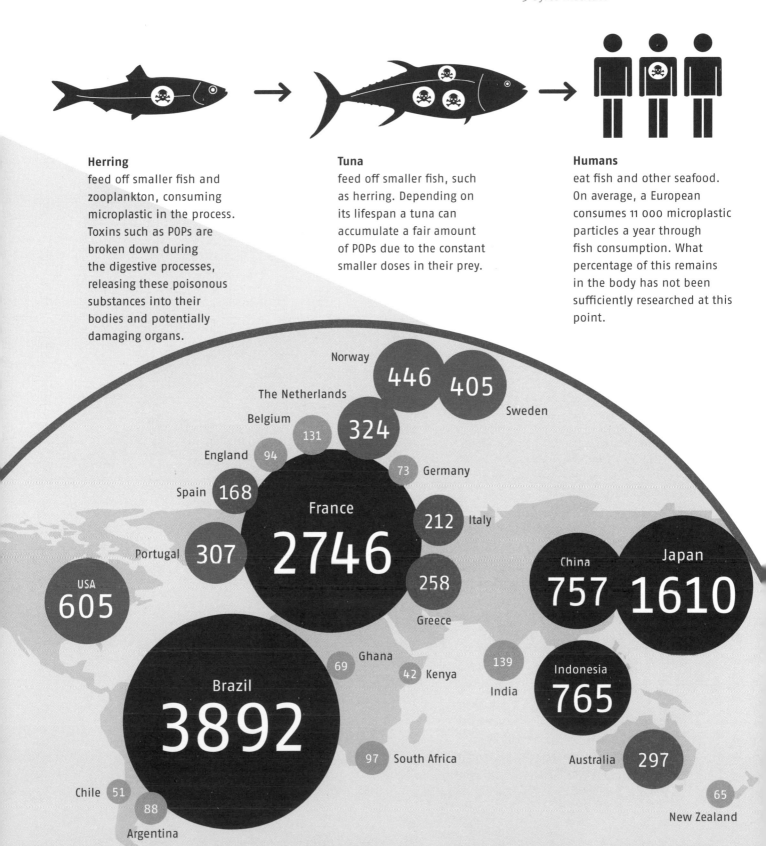

Herring
feed off smaller fish and zooplankton, consuming microplastic in the process. Toxins such as POPs are broken down during the digestive processes, releasing these poisonous substances into their bodies and potentially damaging organs.

Tuna
feed off smaller fish, such as herring. Depending on its lifespan a tuna can accumulate a fair amount of POPs due to the constant smaller doses in their prey.

Humans
eat fish and other seafood. On average, a European consumes 11 000 microplastic particles a year through fish consumption. What percentage of this remains in the body has not been sufficiently researched at this point.

Norway 446   405
Sweden

The Netherlands
Belgium   131
England   94   324

Germany   73

Spain   168

France
2746

Portugal   307

Italy   212

USA
605

Greece   258

Brazil
3892

Ghana   69
Kenya   42

India   139

China
757

Japan
1610

Indonesia
765

South Africa   97

Australia   297

Chile   51

Argentina   88

New Zealand   65

Where do the toxic substances in the oceans come from?

The oceans are constantly being contaminated by pollutants from the atmosphere, rivers and environment in general. Persistent organic pollutants (POPs) can be found in all physical states and pose a serious global threat, because they are broken down extremely slowly in nature and can consequently accumulate easily in humans, animals and plants.

Among the POPs are polychlorinated biphenyls (PCB), dioxins such as PCDD and PCDF, and nonylphenol (NP). PCB was first produced commercially in the 1930s as a coolant for refrigerators, hydraulic fluid in machines, and as a heat-conveying fluid for many other industrial purposes. Later it was mixed in as plasticizer in synthetics, and as a flame retardant in varnishes, paints and glues. Only in the 1980s did it become clear how quickly the toxin could enter the environment through air and waste water, accumulating within organisms and spreading illnesses such as cancer, deformations and even death. Despite its production becoming illegal following the Stockholm Agreements of 1989, half of all PCB-containing machines are still being used to this day. Especially third-world and fast-developing nations are responsible for improper disposal. Thus PCB continues to enter ground waters through the soil, rivers and oceans.

"Dioxins" is a collective term describing chemically similar chlorine-containing dioxins and furanes. They are formed when substances containing chlorine are burned at temperatures above 300°C (570°F). The dioxins enter the atmosphere largely when trash is burned, in metal production, but also through volcanic eruptions and forest fires.

Dioxin emissions have declined dramatically in industrial nations due to technological advancements and strict emission guidelines. Still, dioxin contamination has been found in foods such as fish, meat, dairy products and eggs. The dangerously toxic dioxins remain in the soil and the sediments of rivers and oceans for decades.

Nonylphenoles (NP) are contained in cosmetics, shower gels, washing and laundry liquids, disposable packaging and spray paint, for example. These chemicals enter the soil, rivers and oceans through waste waters and rain drainage. They present a threat to humans and animals alike. Rivers with high nonylphenole concentrations see a decrease in fish populations, and experiments in laboratories have shown that they inhibit fertility and change the fishes' social behaviour.

Sources: Günther et al. (2002), Rios (2007), UBA (2015), UBA (2003)

Plasticizer (PCB)   Dioxins (PCDD) + (PCDF)   Nonylphenol (NP)

Persistent organic pollutants (POPs)

Chemical weapons in the deep seas

Canada
In 1947 the military dumped an undisclosed amount of mustard gas and phosgene 2500 m (8000 ft) below the surface of the ocean about 160 km (100 mi) west of Vancouver Island.

Germany
In 1946 the allied forces ordered 170 000 tons of chemical ammunition to be dumped into the North Sea and 65 000 into the Baltic, among them neurotoxins and choking agents.

Tabun + Phosphen

Hawaii
In 1944/45 the US military disposed of 16 000 mustard gas bombs, 4220 tons of cyanide and 29 tons of mustard gas 8 km (5 mi) south of Pearl Harbour. In 1945 and 1948, 2600 tons of mustard gas, 1225 cyanogen chloride bombs, 15 000 mustard gas bombs and 31 mustard gas grenades were disposed of west of Waianae.

USA
From 1964 until the early 70s, millions of tons of chemical weapons were disposed of by the US in 74 operations, mostly in coastal regions. In the CHASE operations (cut holes and sink 'em), ships loaded with chemical ammunition were made to sink.

Sources: Bearden (2007), Böttcher (2011), CEDRE (2016), CNS (2012), DoD (2010), OSPAR (2015)

Nearly every day between 2009 and 2013, chemical weapons were found in the North and Baltic Seas, as well as in the north east Atlantic. In 2500 cases they were caught in fishing nets at the bottom of the sea or washed up on beaches.

Japan
After World War II, between 1945 and 1952, the US military disposed of chemical weapons off the coast of Japan at 1000 m below the surface. The type and amount of chemicals are undocumented.

New Caledonia
In 1945 the US military disposed of 243 tons of artillery grenades loaded with poisonous chemicals.

Australia
In 1948 approximately 1600 to 2100 tons of chemical weapons from an Australian weapons depot were dumped off King Island.

The US Department of Defense (DoD) reported on 74 cases of "disposing" chemical weapons in the oceans from 1918 well into the 1970s. There is no detailed documentation concerning how many of these weapons were dumped, and where. In many cases, they were already leaking or burst under water during the disposal process or as they hit the bottom of the ocean.

Germany, Japan, Australia and Canada have also disposed of chemical weapons in the ocean, and in Germany too there is no clear documentation of the nature and proportions of these sunken munitions: the "Dangerous munitions waste in the ocean" working group estimates that until 1946 about 1.8 million tons of ammo were dumped, 235 000 tons of which are said to be chemical. Until 1958 fishermen and waste disposal organisations recovered at least 250 000 tons of munition. Fishermen in the North Sea continue to find such weaponry in their nets. From 1945 to 1957, at least 168 people died during the disposal or recovery of such materials. Up to 2008 there have been 262 injured, though the number has fallen to approximately five a year since 1980.

It takes ten to 400 years for the chemicals to be released as a result of the ammunition rusting—depending on its nature and composition. These highly toxic chemicals include arsenic, lead, cyanide, mustard gas and mercury. Some neurotoxins are rendered virtually harmless when dissolved in water. However, mustard gas, for example, does not dissolve in water, and remains seriously toxic to marine lifeforms as well as fishermen.

The consequences that these different chemicals have on our marine ecosystems have yet to be adequately studied.

Radioactivity in the ocean

Atomic bombs tested in the ocean
Radioactive waste disposed of in the ocean

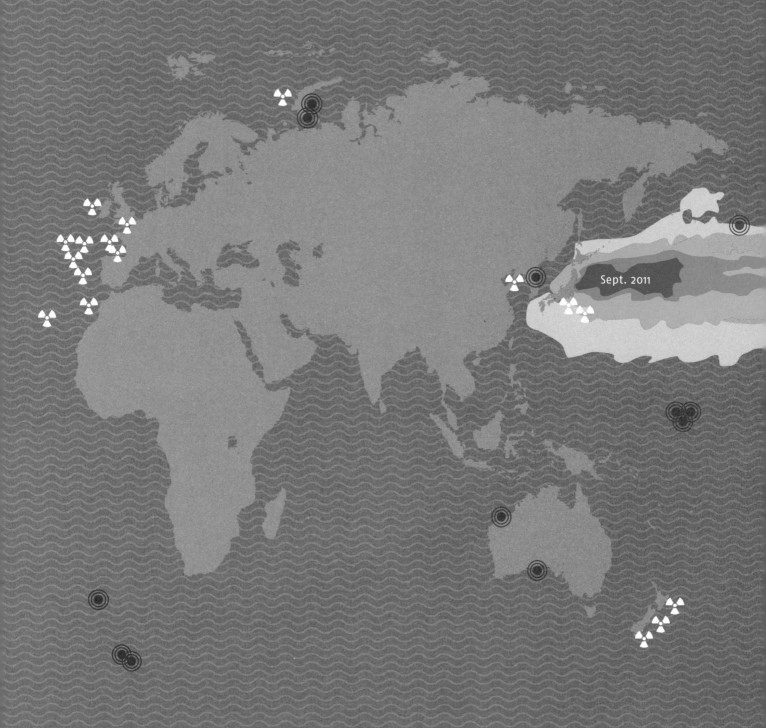

Sept. 2011

Sources: Calmet (1989), DOE (1994), Rossi et al. (2013), CTBTO (2017)

Concentration
of radioactivity
caused by Fukushima
in becquerel per
cubic metre (Bq/35ft³)

September 2011   1000–10 000 Bq/m³   50–1000 Bq/m³   3–50 Bq/m³

April 2014   100–50 Bq/m³   50–3 Bq/m³

April 2014

The first radioactive waste to have
been disposed of in the ocean was in
California in 1946, and the first atomic
bomb tests were carried out on the
Bikini Islands. These were followed by
2040 orchestrated explosions, of which
over 1000 were initiated by the US,
193 by the French—among others in
the Mururoa and Fangataufa atolls of
French Polynesia. In addition, tests have
been conducted by Russia, China, India,
Pakistan and, most recently, North
Korea, testing nuclear weapons both
above and below ground.

Accidents at nuclear power plants
also leak large amounts of radioactivity
into the environment, such as the
Sellafield reactor fire in 1957 or the
Chernobyl meltdown in 1986, where,
after an explosion and meltdown, great
amounts of radioactivity escaped into
the atmosphere and spread into the
soil and rivers, as well as the North,
Baltic and Adriatic Seas, by ways of
dry deposition and rainfall. In 2011,
a tsunami led to an explosion and
partial meltdown at the nuclear power
plant in Fukushima. Millions of tons
of radioactively contaminated coolant
leaked into the North Pacific. Satellite
technology and scientists from around
the world meticulously observed how
small doses reached the coast of North
America in 2014.

*One becquerel is defined as the activity of a quantity
of radioactive material in which one nucleus decays per second.

Fukushima and the marine ecosystem

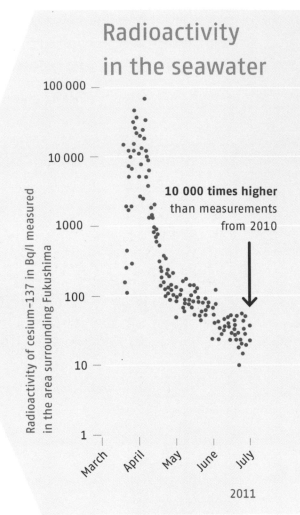

Radioactivity in the seawater

100 000

10 000

10 000 times higher than measurements from 2010

1000

Radioactivity of cesium-137 in Bq/l measured in the area surrounding Fukushima

100

10

1

March April May June July

2011

On March 11, 2011, the largest amount of radio-active substances to date leaked into the ocean. The cause for this was an earthquake that produced a tsunami wave up to 15 m (15 ft) high, which flooded the nuclear reactor at Fukushima Daiichi. After several explosions, reactors 1 to 3—which were in a state of meltdown—were cooled down with ocean water as an immediate emergency measure. This water flowed right back into the ocean. Large amounts of radioactive substances contaminated the air, soil and water and about 170 000 people were evacuated. The creatures of the coastal area were particularly affected; especially those living on the seabed, because radioactive substances accumulate in the sediment at high speed, causing it to be even more radioactive than the surrounding waters, where contamination is diluted thanks to the currents.

In the ocean, the most common radioactive element is cesium-137 with a half-life of approximately 30 years. Right after the meltdown, 50 million Bq/l were found in the waters off the Japanese coast. Later in 2011 it was 4500 Bq/l, further reducing to between 77 and 200 Bq/l in 2012. Though the values have remained fairly constant since then, they have never reached their pre-meltdown levels of 2 Bq/l. This proves that the groundwater and rain, or leaking tanks, continue to seep radio-active contamination into the Pacific.

On the North American cost, the average reading was 11 Bq/l, putting it well below the limit deemed safe for drinking water in the USA (1200 Bq/l).

August 2011
Pacific blue fin tuna are migratory fishes that spawn off the coast of Japan and then migrate 10 000 km (6200 mi) across the Pacific to the US coast. In a comparative study, tuna in San Diego was found to have a level of cesium-137 contamination that was ten times higher.

May 2012
The seabed in the coastal region off Fukushima is estimated to have stored 95 terabecquerel of cesium. Species living on the ocean floor, and also plankton, are consequently subject to much higher levels of contamination the longer they continue to consume organisms from the sediment.

Sediment radioactivity

measured around Fukushima

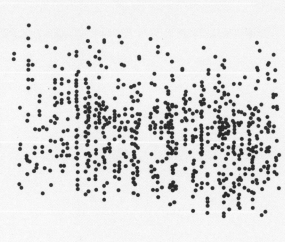

Radioactivity of cesium-137 in Bq/kg (dry weight)

March 2011 · May · July · September · November · January 2012 · March · May · July · September

Cesium-137 has a half-life of about 30 years. The body treats it like potassium and thus stores it in muscles, kidneys, liver and bone cells.

February 21, 2013
The record: 740 000 becquerel of cesium per kilogram (2.2lb) were measured in a greenling. The fish was caught near the damaged Fukushima reactor. The global cesium limit lies at 600 becquerel, though the Japanese limit was adjusted to 1250 becquerel after the accident.

November 17, 2013
12 400 becquerel of cesium-137 per kilogram (2.2lb) were measured in a red porgy caught 37 kilometres (23mi) south of Fukushima.

Migration routes
Many species migrate throughout the entire Pacific, from spawning grounds near Japan all the way to food-rich environments such as California or Alaska.

Sources: Kanda (2012), Madigan (2012), McIntyre (2010), NSF (2011), Pacchioli (2013), WHOI (2016)

The biggest oil spills 1901–2016

Persian Gulf

During the Gulf War, Iraqi soldiers opened the valves of the Sea Island Oil Terminal, while the US military simultaneously attacked Iraqi oil tanks. Approximately 1 million tons of crude oil were spilled, spreading to and contaminating the coasts of South Kuwait and Saudi Arabia.

USA

The largest oil spill in history took place near Kern County, California, in 1909: Approximately 1 227 600 tons of oil seeped into the environment due to a drill leak.

USA

In April 2010 the Deepwater Horizon oil rig lost about 470 779 tons of heavy oil in a drill leak.

Sources: CEDRE (2016), Maribus (2010), WHOI (2011)

1 litre (1 pint) of oil can contaminate up to
1 million litres (1m pints) of drinking water. Every
year approximately 2.6 billion litres (5.5 bn pints)
of oil leak into the oceans.

The sources

of the oil seeping into our oceans
are disputed. Here are two
different scientific estimates

**Woods Hole
Oceanographic
Institution**

**World Ocean
Review**

Japan
In November 1974, a tanker
collision caused about
52 836 tons of oil to be
spilled into the sea in Tokyo
Bay right off Honshu Island.

Natural sources
oil seeping up
from the seabed

47%

5

Shipping
from tank cleaning and
maintenance, for example

24

35

**Waste water,
the atmosphere and
drilling platforms**

19

45

South Africa
In June 1983 a fire on
Spanish tanker Castillo de
Bellver caused 250 000 tons
of light oil to be spilled off
the coast by Saldanha Bay.

Tanker spills

10

10

Undefined sources

5

Oil damage in organisms

Oil spill consequences
Wind and waves spread the oil. It evaporates on the surface of the water, and bacteria who eat oil and occur naturally in the oceans consume certain components of the oil. They metabolise light oils quicker than heavy oil.

Plankton + fish eggs
Upon contact with oil, these fragile micro-organisms as well as fish eggs die immediately or suffer serious deformities.

Plants
Flora is also severely damaged by oil. Sea grass can die off, while resistant algae spread. Giant sea turtles and manatees can become ill or die as a consequence of consuming contami-nated sea grass.

The food chain and spread of disease after oil pollution

Humans
When humans drink water or eat foods contaminated with oil it can cause cancer, liver and respiratory diseases.

Little fish
Many smaller species feed off plankton. When they eat oil-infested plank-ton or get caught in an oil spill, they either die immediately or fall prey to serious diseases such as cardiac dysrhythmia, and reproductive and liver dysfunction. In addition, subsequent generations tend to become smaller.

Pelicans
They sit and float on the surface of the water, making them particu-larly vulnerable to oil slicks: when attempting to groom their plumage, feed or breathe, oil enters their system, causing organ damage. If their plumage is badly gummed up, they can drown.

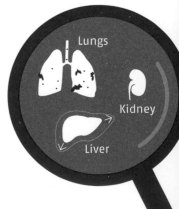

Lungs

Kidney

Liver

A sea turtle as an example

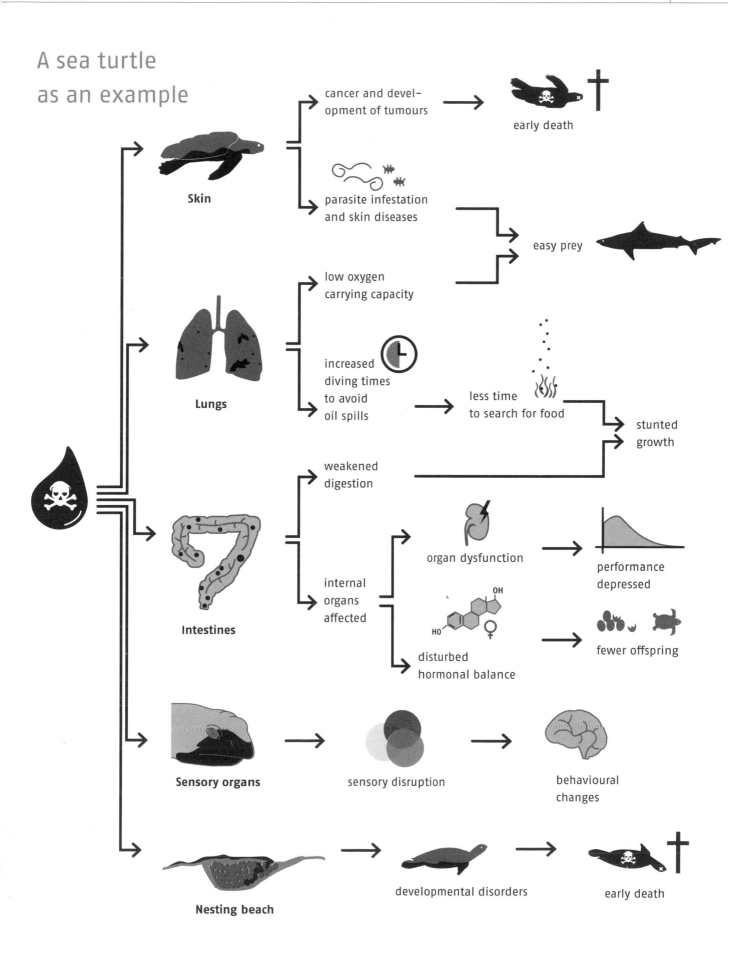

Skin
- cancer and development of tumours → early death
- parasite infestation and skin diseases → easy prey

Lungs
- low oxygen carrying capacity → easy prey
- increased diving times to avoid oil spills → less time to search for food → stunted growth

Intestines
- weakened digestion → stunted growth
- internal organs affected
  - organ dysfunction → performance depressed
  - disturbed hormonal balance → fewer offspring

Sensory organs → sensory disruption → behavioural changes

Nesting beach → developmental disorders → early death

Sources: FWS (2010), NOAA (2010)

"We humans
place an increasing burden
on the oceans. A disturbing
example visible to everyone
is plastic pollution. Other stress factors
include pollution by oil,
radioactivity and fertilisers.
Moreover, the oceans
suffer from global warming.
How much longer can
marine ecosystems cope
with these stressors?
Should the ecosystems collapse,
this too would affect us.
The sinners themselves would
become the victims."

Prof Mojib Latif,
author 'Climate Change: the Point of No Return'

Sources

Chapter 1 Climate change

010 | 011   Heinrich Böll Stiftung (HBS) (2017): Meeresatlas 2017. Daten und Fakten über unseren Umgang mit dem Ozean
https://www.boell.de/de/2017/04/25/meeresatlas-daten-und-fakten-ueber-unseren-umgang-mit-dem-ozean (01.06.2017)

014 | 015   Jouzel, J., Masson-Delmotte, V., Cattani, O., Dreyfus, G., Falourd, S., et al. (2007): Orbital and Millennial Antarctic Climate Variability over the Past 800 000 Years. Science Vol. 317, No. 5839, 793-797, 10 August 2007. doi: 10.1126/science.1141038

Maribus (2010): World Ocean Review – Mit den Meeren leben (S. 10). http://worldoceanreview.com (03.06.2016)

NASA (2015): Featured Article: How is Today's Warming Different from the Past?
http://earthobservatory.nasa.gov/Features/GlobalWarming/page3.php (03.06.2016)

016 | 017   EPA (2014): Climate Change Indicators in the United States: Ocean Heat. http://www.epa.gov/climatechange/indicators

Gleckler, P.J., Durack, P.J., Stouffer, R.J., Johnson, G.C., Forest, C.E. (2016): Industrial-era global ocean heat uptake doubles in recent decades. Nature Climate Change 18th January 2016. doi: 10.1038/nclimate2915

IPCC (2013): Climate Change 2013: The Physical Science Basis. http://www.ipcc.ch/report/ar5/wg1/ (14.04.2017)

018 | 019   ARC Centre of Excellence, Coral Reef Studies (ARC) (2016): Heat sickens corals in global bleaching event.
https://www.coralcoe.org.au/media-releases/heat-sickens-corals-in-global-bleaching-event (14.04.2017)

IPCC (2014): Synthesis Report, Fifth Assessment Report. https://www.ipcc.ch/report/ar5/syr/ (14.04.2017)

Neuheimer, A.B., Hartvig, M., Heuschele, J., Hylander, S., Kiørboe, T., et al. (2015): Adult and offspring size in the ocean over 17 orders of magnitude follows two life history strategies. Ecology, 96: 3303–3311. doi: 10.1890/14-2491.1

Vergés, A., et al. (2014): The tropicalization of temperate marine ecosystems: climate-mediated changes in herbivory and community phase shifts. Proc. R. Soc. B 281: 20140846. http://dx.doi.org/10.1098/rspb.2014.0846 (03.06.2016)

XL Catlin Seaview Survey (2016): Coral Reefs. http://catlinseaviewsurvey.com/science/coral-reefs (03.06.2016)

020 | 021   IGBP, IOC, SCOR (2013): Ozeanversauerung. Zusammenfassung für Entscheidungsträger Third Symposium on the Ocean in a High-CO2 World. http://www.igbp.net/download/18.2fc4e526146d4c130b72cf/1411549163212/OzeanversauerungZfE.pdf (14.04.2017)

Maribus (2010): World Ocean Review – Mit den Meeren leben. http://worldoceanreview.com (03.06.2016)

Climate Central (CC) (2010): Ocean Acidification Process.
http://www.climatecentral.org/gallery/graphics/ocean-acidification-process (03.06.2016)

NOAA (2016): Earth System Research Laboratory. Global Monitoring Division (/gmd/) https://www.esrl.noaa.gov (01.06.2017)

022 | 023   Maribus (2010): World Ocean Review – Mit den Meeren leben. http://worldoceanreview.com (03.06.2016)

NASA (2012): Satellites See Unprecedented Greenland Ice Sheet Surface Melt.
http://www.nasa.gov/topics/earth/features/greenland-melt.html (03.06.2016)

Rahmstorf, S., Box, E., Feulner, G., et al. (2015): Exceptional twentieth-century slowdown in Atlantic Ocean overturning circulation. Nature Climate Change, 23. März 2015. doi: 10.1038/nclimate2554

024 | 025   IPCC (2014): Synthesis Report, Fifth Assessment Report. https://www.ipcc.ch/report/ar5/syr/ (14.04.2017)

Maribus (2010): World Ocean Review – Mit den Meeren leben. http://worldoceanreview.com (15.03.2016)

Pollard, D., DeConto, R.M. (2016): Contribution of Antarctica to past and future sea-level rise. Nature.
http://dx.doi.org/10.1038/nature17145 (06.06.2016)

Vermeer, M., Rahmstorf, S. (2009): Global sea level linked to global temperature. PNAS.
http://www.pnas.org/content/106/51/21527.full.pdf (14.04.2017)

Chapter 2 Loss of biological diversity

030 | 031   Mittermeier, R.A., Turner, W.R., Larsen, F.W., Brooks, T.M., Gascon, C. (2011): Global biodiversity conservation: the critical role of hotspots. Springer, Heidelberg

Kieneke, A., Schmidt-Rhaesa, A., Hochberg, R. (2015): New species of Cephalodasys (Gastrotricha, Macrodasyida) from the Caribbean Sea with a determination key to species of the genus. http://dx.doi.org/10.11646/zootaxa.3947.3.4 (01.06.2017)

William, D., et al. (2016): Grammatonotus brianne, a new callanthiid fish from Philippine waters, with short accounts of two other Grammatonotus from the Coral Triangle. http://doi.org/10.11646/zootaxa.4173.3.7

Poulsen, J.Y., et al. (2016): Preservation Obscures Pelagic Deep-Sea Fish Diversity. Doubling the Number of Sole-Bearing Opisthoproctids and Resurrection of the Genus Monacoa (Opisthoproctidae, Argentiniformes). PLoS ONE Vol. 11, No. 8: e0159762.

Maribus (2010): World Ocean Review – Mit den Meeren leben. http://worldoceanreview.com (03.06.2016)

032 | 033   Abdulla, A., et al. (2013): Marine natural heritage and the World Heritage list. Interpretation of World Heritage criteria in marine systems, analysis of biogeographic representation of sites, and a roadmap for addressing gaps. IUCN, Gland, Schweiz

International Union for Conservation of Nature (IUCN) (2017): The IUCN Red List of Threatened Species. http://www.iucnredlist.org (17.03.2017)

034 | 035   Maribus (2010): World Ocean Review – Mit den Meeren leben. http://worldoceanreview.com (15.03.2016)

Stramma, L., Schmidt, S., Levin, L.A., Johnson, G.C. (2010): Ocean oxygen minima expansions and their biological impacts. http://www.elsevier.com/locate/dsri (15.03.2016)

NODC, NOAA (2005): World Ocean Atlas 2005. IRI/LDEO Climate Data Library, Columbia University. http://iridl.ldeo.columbia.edu/

036 | 037   Australian Government Department of the Environment (AGDE) (2016): Commonwealth Marine Reserves Review. Goals and Principles. http://www.environment.gov.au/marinereservesreview/goals-principles (03.06.2016)

UNEP-WCMC, IUCN (2016): Protected Planet Report 2016. UNEP-WCMC und IUCN: Cambridge, UK and Gland, Schweiz. https://wdpa.s3.amazonaws.com/Protected_Planet_Reports/2445%20Global%20Protected%20Planet%202016_WEB.pdf

Sciberras, M., Jenkins, S.R., Mant, R., Kaiser, M.J., Hawkins, S.J., Pullin, A.S. (2015): Evaluating the relative conservation value of fully and partially protected marine areas. Fish and Fisheries, Vol. 16: 58-77. doi: 10.1111/faf.12044

Chapter 3   Overfishing

042 | 043   FAO (2016): The State of World Fisheries and Aquaculture. http://www.fao.org/3/a-i5555e.pdf (17.02.2017)

Pauly, D., Zeller, D. (2016): Catch reconstructions reveal that global marine fisheries catches are higher than reported and declining. Nature Communications. doi: 10.1038/ncomms10244

044 | 045   Watson, R., Zeller, D., Pauly, D. (2012): Spatial expansion of EU and non-EU fishing fleets into the global ocean 1950 to present. The sea around us-Project, Fish Centre Univ. British Columbia, Kanada, und World Wildlife Fund (WWF)

046 | 047   EU Fishing Fleet Register (2016). http://ec.europa.eu/fisheries/fleet/index.cfm

Greenpeace (2014): Fish Fairly. http://www.greenpeace.de/fairfischen

Shipping companies (2017): Havfisk, Norway. http://www.havfisk.no/en (22.11.2017)

Parlevliet en Van der Plas B.V., Netherlands. http://parlevliet-vanderplas.nl/ (22.11.2017)

048 | 049   International Seafood Sustainability Foundation (ISSF) (2017): Fishing Methods – An Overview. http://iss-foundation.org/about-tuna/fishing-methods (21.03.2017)

Seafish Fisheries Development Centre (2015): Basic Fishing Methods. A comprehensive guide to commercial fishing methods. http://www.seafish.org/media/publications/BFM_August_2015_update.pdf (14.04.2017)

050 | 051   Preston, G.L., et al. (1999): Techniques de pêche profonde pour les Iles du Pacifique. Manuel à l'intention des Pêcheurs. Secrétariat général de la Communauté du Pacifique. http://www.reefbase.org/pacific/pub_E0000001373.aspx (14.04.2017)

052 | 053   FAO (2016): The State of World Fisheries and Aquaculture. http://www.fao.org/3/a-i5555e.pdf (17.02.2017)

ISSF (2017): Status of the World Fisheries for Tuna. ISSF Technical Report 2017-02. http://iss-foundation.org/knowledge-tools/technical-and-meeting-reports (14.04.2017)

054 | 055   Clarke, S.C., Harley, S.J., Hoyle, S.D., Rice J.S. (2007): Population trends in Pacific Oceanic sharks and the utility of regulations on shark finning. Oceanic Fisheries Program, Secretariat of the Pacific Community, B.P. D5,98848, Noum'ea CEDEX, Neukaledonien

European Commission (EC) (2011): Public Consultation on the Amendment of Council Regulation on the Removal of Fins of Sharks http://ec.europa.eu/dgs/maritimeaffairs_fisheries/consultations/shark_finning_ban/consultation_document_en.pdf (14.04.2017)

FAO (2014): The State of World Fisheries and Aquaculture. http://www.fao.org/3/a-i3720e.pdf (14.04.2017)

IUCN Shark Specialist Group (2003): IUCN Information Paper. Shark Finning. http://www.uicnmed.org/web2007/CD2003/conten/pdf/shark_FINAL.pdf (14.04.2017)

WildAid (2014): Evidence of declines in shark fin demand China. http://wildaid.org/sites/default/files/SharkReport_spread_final_08.07.14.pdf (03.06.2016)

056 | 057 ceta-base (2012): Tracking Taiji. Live Capture & Export Data from Drive Fisheries. Ceta-Base: Online Marine Mammal Inventory. 2012

Sea Shepherd (2016): Cove Guardians. Operation Infinite Patience. Dolphin Defense Campaign. http://www.seashepherd.org/cove-guardians/facts.html (03.06.2016)

058 | 059 Brewer, D., et al. (2006): The impact of turtle excluder devices and bycatch reduction devices on diverse tropical marine communities in Australia's northern prawn trawl fishery. Fisheries Research. Vol. 81, Issues 2–3, November 2006, 176–188

Haine, O.S., Garvey, J.R. (2005): Northern Prawn Fishery Data Summary 2005. Logbook Program, Australian Fisheries Management Authority. http://www.afma.gov.au/wp-content/uploads/2010/06/NPF-Data-Summary-2005-2.pdf?afba77 (21.03.2017)

Lewison, R.L., et al. (2014): Global patterns of marine mammal, seabird, and sea turtle bycatch reveal taxa-specific and cumulative megafauna hotspots. PNAS, 2014 Apr 8; 111(14): 5271–5276. http://www.ncbi.nlm.nih.gov/pmc/articles/PMC3986184 (03.06.2016)

Consortium for Wildlife Bycatch Reduction (CWBR) (2017). http://www.bycatch.org (03.06.2016)

060 | 063 Maribus (2013): World Ocean Review 2, Die Zukunft der Fische – die Fischerei der Zukunft. http://worldoceanreview.com (03.06.2016)

FAO (2014): The State of World Fisheries and Aquaculture. http://www.fao.org/3/a-i3720e.pdf (14.04.2017)

064 | 065 Department of Fisheries and Oceans Canada (DFO) (2013): Aquaculture in Canada: Integrated Multi-Trophic Aquaculture (IMTA) http://publications.gc.ca/collections/collection_2013/mpo-dfo/Fs45-4-2013-eng.pdf (14.04.2017)

Maribus (2013): World Ocean Review 2, Die Zukuft der Fische – die Fischerei der Zukunft.

066 | 067 Agnew, D.J., Pearce, J., Pramod, G., Peatman, T., Watson, R., Beddington, J.R., Pitcher, T.J. (2009): Estimating the Worldwide Extent of Illegal Fishing. PLoS ONE 4(2):e4570. doi:10.1371/journal.pone.0004570

Maribus (2013): World Ocean Review 2, Die Zukunft der Fische – die Fischerei der Zukunft.

United Nations Conference on Trade and Development (UNCTAD) (2013): Review of maritime transport 2013 http://unctad.org/en/PublicationsLibrary/rmt2013_en.pdf (14.04.2017)

Chapter 4 Ocean-based industries

072 | 073 CIA (2015): The World Factbook. https://www.cia.gov/library/publications/the-world-factbook/rankorder/2241rank.html (25.01.2016)

U.S. Energy Information Administration (EIA) (2017): Short-Term Energy Outlook – Global Liquid Fuels. https://www.eia.gov/outlooks/steo/report/global_oil.cfm (14.04.2017)

OECD/IEA (2016): Key World Energy Statistics. https://www.iea.org/publications/freepublications/publication/key-world-energy-statistics.html (14.04.2017)

Global Wind Energy Council (GWEC) (2016): Global Wind Statistics 2015.

Quest Offshore (2013): The Economic Benefits of Increasing U.S. Access to Offshore Oil and Natural Gas Resources in the Atlantic. http://www.api.org/~/media/files/oil-and-natural-gas/exploration/offshore/atlantic-ocs/offshore-state-fl.pdf (14.04.2017)

074 | 075 European Wind Energy Association (EWEA) (2016): Offshore statistics. http://www.ewea.org/statistics/offshore-statistics (18.03.2016)

Gill, A.B. (2005): Offshore renewable energy. Ecological implications of generating electricity in the coastal zone. Journal of Applied Ecology. http://onlinelibrary.wiley.com/doi/10.1111/j.1365-2664.2005.01060.x/abstract (14.04.2017)

James, V. (2013): Marine renewable energy: A global review of the extent of marine renewable energy developments, the developing technologies and possible conservation implications for cetaceans. http://uk.whales.org/sites/default/files/wdc-marine-renewable-energy-report.pdf (14.04.2017)

Langhamer, O. (2012): Artificial reef effect in relation to offshore renewable energy conversion: State of the art. The Scientific World Journal Vol. 2012. http://dx.doi.org/10.1100/2012/386713 (18.03.2016)

Wahlberg, M., Westerberg, H. (2005): Hearing in fish and their reactions to sounds from offshore wind farms. Marine Ecology Progress Series, Vol. 288. http://www.int-res.com/abstracts/meps/v288/p295-309 (14.04.2017)

Sources

Zeiler, M., Dahlke, C., Nolte, N. (2005): Offshore-Windparks in der ausschließlichen Wirtschaftszone von Nord- und Ostsee. Promet, Jahrg. 31, Nr. 1. http://www.bsh.de/de/Meeresnutzung/Wirtschaft/Windparks/Windparks/Literatur/Genehmigungsverfahren_fuer_Offshore-Windparks.pdf (14.04.2017)

076 | 077   World Energy Council (WEC) (2013): 2013 Survey of Energy Resources.
https://www.worldenergy.org/publications/2013/world-energy-resources-2013-survey (14.04.2017)

Ocean Energy Systems (OES) (2014): 2014 Annual Report. Implementing Agreement on Ocean Energy Systems.
https://report2014.ocean-energy-systems.org (14.04.2017)

078 | 079   GEOMAR (2016): Massivsulfide – Rohstoffe aus der Tiefsee.
http://www.geomar.de/fileadmin/content/service/presse/public-pubs/massivsulfide_2016_de_web.pdf

Maribus (2014): World Ocean Review 3. Rohstoffe aus dem Meer – Chancen und Risiken.
http://worldoceanreview.com (14.04.2017)

Rona, P.A. (2003): Resources of the sea floor. Science. http://science.sciencemag.org/content/299/5607/673 (14.04.2017)

Umweltbundesamt (UBA) (2013): Tiefseebergbau und andere Nutzungsarten der Tiefsee.
http://www.umweltbundesamt.de/themen/wasser/gewaesser/meere/nutzung-belastungen/tiefseebergbau-andere-nutzungsarten-der-tiefsee (06.06.2016)

United Nations Environmental Programme (UNEP) (2013): Wealth in the oceans: Deep sea mining on the horizon? UNEP Global Environmental Alter Service. http://www.unep.org/geas (06.06.2016)

080 | 081   Bundesanstalt für Geowissenschaften und Rohstoffe (BGR) (2015): Abbau-/Fördertechnik Massivsulfide und Manganknollen

Devold, H. (2013): Oil and gas production handbook. An introduction to oil and gas production, transport, refining and petrochemical industry. http://resourcelists.rgu.ac.uk/items/6D0FE355-9C5F-56B1-3D6C-CD82B8041428.html (14.04.2017)

Maribus (2014): World Ocean Review 3. Rohstoffe aus dem Meer – Chancen und Risiken.

082 | 083   Kommission der Europäischen Gemeinschaften, Statistisches Amt (KEG) (1970): Der Seeverkehr der Länder der Gemeinschaft. 1955, 1960 und 1967 – Eine statistische Studie, Brüssel-Luxemburg, Mai 1970

NABU (2014): Luftschadstoffemissionen von Containerschiffen. Hintergrundpapier. https://www.nabu.de/imperia/md/content/nabude/verkehr/140623-nabu-hintergrundpapier_containerschifftransporte.pdf (14.04.2017)

United Nations Conference on Trade and Development (UNCTAD) (2016): Review of Maritime Transport.
http://unctad.org/en/PublicationsLibrary/rmt2016_en.pdf (14.04.2017)

084 | 085   Marine Traffic (2016): Live map. http://www.marinetraffic.com (23.02.2016)

Corbett, J.J., et al.(2007): Mortality from ship emissions. A global assessment.
http://pubs.acs.org/doi/full/10.1021/es071686z (01.06.2017)

086 | 087   Jasny, M., Reynolds, J., Horowitz, C., Wetzler, A. (2005): Sounding the Depths II: The rising toll of sonar, shipping and industrial ocean noise on marine life. Natural Resources Defense Council.
http://www.nrdc.org/wildlife/marine/sound/contents.asp (15.03.2016)

Nowacek, S.M., Wells, R.S., Solow, A.R. (2001): Short-term effects of boat traffic on bottlenose dolphins, tursiops truncatus, in Sarasota Bay, Florida, Marine Mammal Science, Vol. 17, No. 4: 673-688 (October 2001)

Schorr, G.S., Falcone, E.A., Moretti, D.J., Andrews, R.D. (2014): First long-term behavioral records from Cuvier's beaked whales (Ziphiuscavirostris) reveal record-breaking dives. PLoS One. Vol. 9, No. 3: e92633. doi: 10.1371/journal.pone.0092633

Veirs, S., Veirs, V., Wood, J.D. (2016): Ship noise extends to frequencies used for echolocation by endangered killer whales. PeerJ 4:e1657. https://doi.org/10.7717/peerj.1657 (14.04.2017)

088 | 089   Andrulewicz, E., Napierska, D., Otremba, Z. (2003): The environmental effects of the installation and functioning of the submarine SwePol Link HVDC transmission line. A case study of the Polish Marine Area of the Baltic Sea. Journal of Sea Research.
http://www.sciencedirect.com/science/article/pii/S1385110103000200 (14.04.2017)

TeleGeography (TG) (2016): Submarine Cable Map. Global Bandwidth Research Service.
http://www.submarinecablemap.com (26.02.2016)

Starosielski, N. (2015): The Undersea Network. Duke University Press. https://www.dukeupress.edu/the-undersea-network (01.06.2017)

Chapter 5 Pollution

094 | 095   Centre for Science and Environment (CSE) (2013): 7th State of India's Environment Report: Excreta Matters.
http://cseindia.org/content/excreta-matters-0 (14.04.2017)

United States Environmental Protection Agency (EPA) (2012): Municipal Solid Waste Generation, Recycling, and Disposal in the United States: Facts and Figures for 2012. https://archive.epa.gov/epawaste/nonhaz/municipal/web/html/ (14.04.2017)

Klein, R.A. (2009): Getting a Grip on Cruise Ship Pollution.
http://www.foe.org/projects/oceans-and-forests/cruise-ships (14.04.2017)

Maribus (2010): World Ocean Review 1 – Mit den Meeren leben. http://worldoceanreview.com (03.06.2016)

Umweltbundesamt (UBA) (2015): Quellen für Mikroplastik mit Relevanz für den Meeresschutz in Deutschland.
https://www.umweltbundesamt.de/sites/default/files/medien/378/publikationen/texte_63_2015_quellen_fuer_mikroplastik_mit_relevanz_fuer_den_meeresschutz_1.pdf (17.12.2017)

United Nations Environment Programme (UNEP) (2005): Marine Litter. An Analytical Overview.
http://www.unep.org/regionalseas/marinelitter/publications/docs/anl_oview.pdf (20.04.2015)

096 | 097   Schlining, K., et al. (2013): Debris in the deep: Using a 22-year video annotation database to survey marine litter in Monterey Canyon, Central California, USA. Monterey Bay Aquarium Research Institute (MBARI)

Plastics Europe (PE) (2016): Plastics. The Facts 2016. An analysis of European plastics production, demand and waste data.
http://www.plasticseurope.org/documents/document/20161014113313-plastics_the_facts_2016_final_version.pdf (14.04.2017)

Subba Reddy, M., et al. (2014): Effect of Plastic Pollution on Environment. Department of Chemistry, S.B.V.R. Aided Degree College, badvel, Kadapa-516227, India. Journal of Chemical and Pharmaceutical Sciences

United Nations Environment Programme (UNEP) (2015): The Plastics Disclosure Project.
http://www.plasticdisclosure.org/about/why-pdp.html (03.06.2016)

World Economic Forum (WEF) (2016): The New Plastics Economy. Rethinking the future of plastics

098 | 099   Eriksen, M., Lebreton, L.C.M., Carson, H.S., Thiel, M., Moore, C.J., Borerro, J.C., et al. (2014):
Plastic pollution in the world's oceans: More than 5 trillion plastic pieces weighing over 250,000 tons afloat at sea. PLoS ONE 9(12): e111913. doi:10.1371/journal.pone.0111913

International Pacific Research Center (IPRC) (2008): Tracking Ocean Debris. IPRC Climate. Newsletter of the International Pacific Research Center. Vol. 8, No. 2. http://iprc.soest.hawaii.edu/newsletters/iprc_climate_vol8_no2.pdf (14.04.2017) World Economic Forum

100 | 101   Eriksen, M., Lebreton, L.C.M., Carson, H.S., Thiel, M., Moore, C.J., Borerro, J.C., et al. (2014):
Plastic pollution in the world's oceans: More than 5 trillion plastic pieces weighing over 250,000 tons afloat at sea. PLoS ONE 9(12): e111913. doi:10.1371/journal.pone.0111913

Greenpeace (GP) (2007): Plastic Debris in the World's Oceans. http://www.greenpeace.org/international/Global/international/planet-2/report/2007/8/plastic_ocean_report.pdf (20.04.2015)

Moore, C. J., Moore, S.L., Leecaster, L.K., Weisberg, S.B. (2001): A comparison of plastic and plankton in the North Pacific Central Gyre. Marine Bulletin Vol. 42, No. 12, 1297-1300. http://www.sciencedirect.com/science/article/pii/S0025326X0100114X (14.04.2017)

Ocean Conservancy, International Coastal Cleanup (ICC) (2010): Trash Travels.
http://act.oceanconservancy.org/images/2010ICCReportRelease_pressPhotos/2010_ICC_Report.pdf (20.04.2015)

Maribus (2010): World Ocean Review – Mit den Meeren leben. http://worldoceanreview.com (20.04.2015)

United Nations Environment Programme (UNEP) (2005): Marine Litter. An Analytical Overview.
http://www.cep.unep.org/content/about-cep/amep/marine-litter-an-analytical-overview/view (14.04.2017)

102 | 103   International Pellet Watch (IPW) (2015): Global Pollution Map. Global Monitoring of Persistent Organic Pollutants (POPs) using Beached Plastic Resin Pellets. http://www.pelletwatch.org/gmap/ (03.06.2016)

Rios, L.M., Moore, C. (2007): Persistent organic pollutants carried by synthetic polymers in the ocean environment. Marine Pollution Bulletin Vol. 54 (2007) 1230–1237. University of the Pacific

Van Cauwenberghe L., Janssen C. (2014): Microplastics in bivalves cultured for human consumption. Environmental Pollution, Vol. 193, 65-70. doi: 10.1016/j.envpol.2014.06.010

104 | 105   Günther, K., Heinke, V., Thiele, B., Kleist, E., Prast, H., Räcker, T. (2002): Endocrine disrupting nonylphenols are ubiquitous in food. Environ. Sci. Technol., http://pubs.acs.org/cgi-bin/doilookup?10.1021/es010199v (03.06.2016)

Sources

Rios, L.M., Moore, C. (2007): Persistent organic pollutants carried by synthetic polymers in the ocean environment. Marine Pollution Bulletin Vol. 54 (2007) 1230–1237. University of the Pacific

Umweltbundesamt (UBA) (2015): Ermittlung von potentiell POP-haltigen Abfällen und Recyclingstoffen. Ableitung von Grenzwerten. http://www.umweltbundesamt.de/publikationen/ermittlung-von-potentiell-pop-haltigen-abfaellen (03.06.2016)

Umweltbundesamt (UBA) (2003): Persistent Organic Pollutants – POPs. http://www.umweltbundesamt.de/sites/default/files/medien/publikation/long/2727.pdf (03.06.2016)

106 | 107   Bearden, D.M., et al. (2007): U.S. disposal of chemical weapons in the ocean: Background and issues for Congress

Böttcher, C., et al. (2011): Munitionsbelastung der deutschen Meeresgewässer. Bestandsaufnahme und Empfehlungen Arbeitsgemeinschaft Bund/Länder-Messprogramm für die Meeresumwelt von Nord- und Ostsee. http://www.munition-im-meer.de (03.06.2016)

Centre of Documentation Research and Experimentation on Accidental Water Pollution (CEDRE) (2016): Munitions dumped at sea. http://wwz.cedre.fr/en/Our-resources/Discharge-at-sea/Munitions-dumped-at-sea (03.06.2016)

James Martin Center for Nonproliferation Studies (CNS) (2012): Chemical weapon munitions dumped at sea: An interactive map. http://www.nonproliferation.org/chemical-weapon-munitions-dumped-at-sea (03.06.2016)

Department of Defense (DoD) (2010): Final Investigation Report HI-05. Hawai'i Undersea Military Munitions Assessment (HUMMA). http://64.78.11.86/uxofiles/enclosures/HI5_Final_Investigation_Report_June2010.pdf (14.04.2017)

OSPAR Commission (2015): Encounters with Chemical and Conventional Munitions 2013. http://www.ospar.org/site/assets/files/7413/assessment_sheet_munitions_2015.pdf (03.06.2016)

108 | 109   Calmet, D.P. (1989): Ocean disposal of radioactive waste: Status report. International Atomic Energy Agency (IAEA). Bulletin 4/1989

U.S. Department of Energy (DOE) (1994): United States Nuclear Tests: July 1945 through September 1992. Document No. DOE/NV-209

Rossi, V., et al. (2013): Multi-decadal projections of surface and interior pathways of the Fukushima Cesium-137 radioactive plume. Deep Sea Research Part I: Oceanographic Research Papers Vol. 80, October 2013, 37–46

Preparatory Commission for the Comprehensive Nuclear-Test-Ban Treaty Organization (CTBTO) (2017): CTBTO world map. Locations of nuclear explosions. http://www.ctbto.org/map/#testing (13.03.2017)

110 | 111   Kanda (2012): Longterm sources: To what extent are marine sediments, coastal groundwater, and rivers a source of ongoing contamination? Tokyo University of Marine Science and Technology. 13 Nov 2012

Madigan, D.J. (2012): Pacific bluefin tuna transport Fukushima-derived radionuclides from Japan to California. PNAS Vol. 109 No. 24, 12. Juni 2012 http://www.pnas.org/content/109/24/9483.abstract (13.04.2017)

McIntyre, A., et al. (2010): Life in the world's oceans. Diversity, distribution and abundance. Chapter 15: A view of the ocean from Pacific predators. Census of Marine Life Maps and Visualization. Verlag Wiley-Blackwell, Hoboken, New Jersey, USA

National Science Foundation (NSF) (2011): Scientists assess radioactivity in the ocean from Japan nuclear power facility. Press Release 11-258. https://www.nsf.gov/news/news_summ.jsp?cntn_id=122542 (13.04.2017)

Pacchioli, D. (2013): How is Fukushima's fallout affecting marine life? Woods Hole Oceanographic Institution. Oceanus Magazine, 2. Mai 2013 http://www.whoi.edu/oceanus/feature/how-is-fukushimas-fallout-affecting-marine-life (13.04.2017)

Wood Hole Oceanographic Institution (WHOI) (2016): Fukushima site still leaking after five years, research shows. http://www.whoi.edu/news-release/fukushima-site-still-leaking (21.03.2016)

112 | 113   Centre of Documentation, Research and Experimentation on Accidental Water Pollution (CEDRE) (2016): Database of spill incidents and threats in waters around the world. http://wwz.cedre.fr/en/Our-resources/Spills (03.06.2016)

Maribus (2010): World Ocean Review 1 – Mit den Meeren leben. http://worldoceanreview.com (03.06.2016)

WHOI (2011): Sources of oil in the ocean.

114 | 115   U.S. Fish & Wildlife Service (FWS) (2010): Effects of oil on wildlife and habitat. https://www.fws.gov/home/dhoilspill/pdfs/dhjicfwsoilimpactswildlifefactsheet.pdf (13.04.2017)

National Oceanographic and Atmospheric Administration (NOAA) (2010): Oil and sea turtles. Biology, planning and response. http://response.restoration.noaa.gov/sites/default/files/Oil_Sea_Turtles.pdf (03.06.2016)

About the Author

 Esther Gonstalla is an award-winning infographic designer, whose work has appeared in German, Japanese and English. Her first book in the series, 'The Atom Book: Radioactive Waste and Lost Atom Bombs' is described as 'one of the most beautiful German books of 2009'. Her next book 'The Climate Book', is now followed by 'The Ocean Book', whose focus is on the state of our oceans and the man-made problems inflicted upon them.
(Her portfolio can be seen at www.erdgeschoss-grafik.de)

Thank you

to all the people who made this book a reality, particularly the scientists:
Prof Hartmut Grassl, Prof Axel Timmermann, Prof Martin Visbeck, Prof Mojib Latif,
Prof Daniel Pauly, Dr Matthias Schaber, Dr Malte Stuecker, Dr Sven Petersen, and
Dr Marcus Eriksen. To the German Ocean Foundation and especially Frank Schweikert
for his specialist support. To my partner, my friends and my family.

"What should the oceans
of the future look like?
And what are you
willing to sacrifice for them?
Don't be afraid to start small.
Every little action counts
and many small actions will lead
to a bigger change.
Eventually."

Esther Gonstalla

The American Pageant

Guidebook